know

0 8 2008

Esquire

things
a man
should
know

about work
and sex

and some things in between

TED ALLEN & SCOTT OMELIANUK

Design by Serg Andreyev, Neuwirth & Associates, Inc.
Back cover photo of Scott Omelianuk by Cara Dubroff

This book was published as two separate books, each with it's own Library of Congress Cataloging-in-Publication Data. The titles were: *Esquire's Things a Man Should Know About Sex*, and *Esquire's Things a Man Should Know About Handshakes, White Lies, and Which Fork Goes Where*.

Library of Congress Cataloging-in-Publication Data
Allen, Ted.
  Esquire things a man should know about work and sex (and some things in between) / Ted Allen and Scott Omelianuk.
      p. cm.
  Rev. ed. of: Esquire's things a man should know about sex. 1st ed. c2001.
  Includes index.
  ISBN 1-58816-214-1
1. Business etiquette. 2. Sex instruction for men. I. Title: Things a man should know about work and sex (and some things in between). II. Omelianuk, Scott. III. Allen, Ted. Esquire's things a man should know about sex. IV. Series: Esquire (New York, N.Y.) V. Title.
  HF5389.A48 2004
  650.–dc_2

                                        2004020055

10 9 8 7 6 5 4 3 2 1

Published by Hearst Books
A Division of Sterling Publishing Co., Inc.
387 Park Avenue South, New York, NY 10016

Esquire is a trademark owned by Hearst Magazines Property, Inc., in USA, and Hearst Communications, Inc., in Canada. Hearst Books is a trademark owned by Hearst Communications, Inc.
www.esquire.com

All Hearst titles are available at a discount when purchasing in quantity for sales promotions or corporate use. Special editions, including personalized covers, excerpts and corporate imprints can be created when purchasing in large quantities. For more information, please call Premium Sales at 212.532.7160 or email specialsales@sterlingpub.com.

Distributed in Canada by Sterling Publishing
℅ Canadian Manda Group, 165 Dufferin Street
Toronto, Ontario, Canada M6K 3H6

Distributed in Australia by Capricorn Link (Australia) Pty. Ltd.
P.O. Box 704, Windsor, NSW 2756 Australia

Printed in the USA
ISBN 1-58816-214-1

contents

introduction

It all begins with the handshake—and thus so shall we.

It launches every great partnership, every brilliant deal, every campaign and treaty and used-car sale. It is the first thing we must do as we stride into each new corner of the world—that is, to make an impression on its occupants—and pressing the flesh is among our first such opportunities.

One such impression might be that you sweat no more than the next guy. Another, so long as there are no weapons in your paw, is that you have no plans to kill anybody just this minute—people never get tired of that. Also favorably regarded is your disinclination to serve as a vector for dysentery, thus, the custom of extending the *right* hand for greeting purposes, reserving the left for germy personal cleansing. It is ironic in these fussy, antibacterial times that some men prefer to shake no hands at all, not even the right one. Among the more famously fastidious is one-time presidential hopeful Donald Trump, who called the custom "barbaric."

Well, it is not barbaric. (Trump, on the other hand . . .) Quite the opposite, in fact. It is the quintessential gesture of masculine civility. And it has persisted, like most time-honored rituals of etiquette and courtesy, arbitrary or odd or archaic though they may seem, because it works.

Etiquette, you could argue, has gotten a bad rap among the putatively rougher sex. The word evokes society mavens, heiresses to breakfast-cereal fortunes, prissy people and their effete, fey, girly functions, mostly weddings and debutante balls. Not so. So very, very not so. No aspect of human endeavor has more byzantine codes of conduct than the business world, and nowhere are the stakes as high—we're not talking here about being dropped from the social register when you make a mistake; we're talking about your no longer being able to afford food. The rituals and conventions of business, they help us project an image of ourselves as smart, traveled, sophisticated, and self-assured. They help everyone know where they stand in your eyes and where you stand in theirs. They allow us to convey to our fellow travelers such things as regard, respect, and friendliness, a sense of prospective sharedness-of-purpose. The handshake, well tendered, it says: You are a pro. I am a pro. We are smart and prepared and not to be trifled with—and now, let us conduct some commerce.

What is perhaps more important: Not only do rules of conduct apply to you, they are your *friend*. Your very good friend. When you know the rules—what not to order at a lunch meeting, how to fire somebody, how to ask for a raise, when to kiss a client (not often)—your knowledge does more than just make you look good to other people. It makes you feel relaxed and comfortable. It becomes second nature, an integral part of your personal style. And that looking good to other people, that comfort in even uncomfortable situations, well, when you've got the same seniority as the other guys, it's *the* thing that helps you get ahead.

Or to put it another way, it helps you attain what Esquire has always helped men attain—that sophistication and confidence that we like to call Man at His Best.

So let us go forth, then, freshly steeled in the face of danger, strong before difficulties, and let us wheel and deal and shape new worlds. Let's sign on the dotted line, and mean it. And just as it all begins, so must in conclude—let us shake on it.

Pleasure doing business with you.

Now onto the good stuff!

things a man should know about **work**

You know, of course, that you want it. Among the many lessons we are taught from birth—before birth, really, what with genes and instinct and all—none is clearer than this: We will spend our lives wanting it. Not merely wanting, of course: craving it, savoring it, salivating at the merest glimmer of the idea of it, verily, by definition, *lusting*. We read books and watch movies and witness the behavior of sultry waitresses and randy single uncles, and one thing we learn for sure is that we must do anything, anything at all—risk prison, jettison friends, beg, shoplift, embezzle, scream, listen to Enya, beg, get religion, change religions, trash careers, shoot hand-tooled shotguns into the starry Indonesian sky, beg, crash the Porsche, sky-dive, seek counseling, borrow, beg, align chakras, drink poison, beg, kill, kill again, be killed, rise from the dead, and most especially, having little recourse remaining, beg—if there is even the slimmest chance that it might result in a little bit of netherly friction, which is to say, sex.

What most men don't know, unfortunately, is how to do it.

Oh, we might think we do, but the writers and researchers of this volume have it on good authority (women) that many of us (men) don't. Even if not one of us (men) will admit it.

We are not taught Word One about performing things sexual, even now, when concerns about polite conversation seem ridiculously quaint. In particular, we men are never schooled in the sorts of things sexual that *women* might enjoy—an important consideration, that, at least among those seeking your more common sexual arrangement of one male and one female. Indeed, who would tell us such things? Dad? Er, *Mom?* Professionally trained and certified health teachers in the primary grades, who all seem to be overweight gym teachers in stretchy pants whose last erection quite possibly occurred on a weekend furlough during the Korean War? Even if these people were willing and able, are they really the ones from whom we'd choose to learn the finer points of, say, toe nibbling?

No. Rather, that would be us. Not in person, of course. But in print, in this book, here.

We have talked to the womenfolk. They have told us many things that you should know. We also have consulted important studies of human sexual behavior, from the classics (Hite, Kinsey, Erica Jong, Snoop Dogg) to the groundbreaking University of Chicago report of 1996, except where we made things up completely. We have argued and debated and arrived at conclusions. We have culled fascinating statistics and lore, because everybody wants to measure himself (sometimes literally) against his peers. And we have tried throughout to keep our sense of humor— because if there's one thing sex should nearly always involve, it is not only warmth and fondness, if not love, but the acceptance of laughter—though never at that moment when your trousers drop.

As they say, birds do it. Bees do it. Even so-and-so's in the trees do it. But how about this: Let us do it (not you and us, but us in a more general sense, of course). Yes, let's do it, but let's do it really, really well.

things a man should know about **sex**

chapter one

First off, here we have some special body language that tells people you have no plans to kill them.

Seeing as how all business starts with the handshake, let us as well: The handshake shall be firm, fast, and free of excess perspiration.

Translation: *Firm* **means a squeeze, but not a hard squeeze.**

Fast means that this squeeze happens in an instant and is not sustained.

As for perspiration, that was discreetly wiped off on your trousers a few seconds ago.

The practice of handshaking arose in part as a good-faith gesture that one's right paw contained no weaponry.

Also, in some cultures, handshaking is reserved for the right hand, whereas, for excellent and hygienic reasons, the most personal of personal cleansing tasks is reserved for the left.

Something to keep in mind when considering the previous note: Not everybody is right-handed— but we digress.

The best handshake: two firm, quick, and confident pumps, followed by release.

People in other cultures shake hands differently.

things a man should know about **work**

Businesspersons in some African countries, for example, tend to retain their grip much longer than businesspersons in the U.S.

Policy for shaking hands with people in other cultures: When in Rome . . .

It's called respect.

Respect for other people, you see (and their prospectively proportional regard for you), is the guiding principle behind all matters of etiquette.

Also: When you know how to behave, you are comfortable, you are relaxed, you are at your best.

Not *that* relaxed: Augmenting the handshake with a brief thumb-wrestle, the knocking of fists atop one another, the "giving" of "five," or any similar flourish is acceptable in a business context only for boxers, fraternity brothers, and members of boy bands.

Extending one's hand as if to shake, then suddenly withdrawing same and smoothing back one's hair: You, Fonzie, are fired.

It is sometimes useful to lend a moderate extra measure of affection to a handshake by bringing up the left hand and patting the shoulder.

Engulfing your colleague's hand with both of yours: if you are a Protestant minister or consoling the widow at a funeral or, of course, Bill Clinton.

The handshake that starts as a handshake but is then used to pull you into a hug: You must decide whether to submit to such affection on a case-by-case basis.

It's usually easiest to just give in and let yourself be hugged.

things a man should know about **work**

Afterward, you can cease all future business activities with promiscuous huggers, unless your business is the recording of hip-hop music.

Or unless you come to realize that you really needed a hug, which you probably did.

When to shake a woman's hand (old school): when she extends hers first.

When to shake a woman's hand (modern view): whenever you would shake any businessperson's hand.

When to kiss the cheek of a businessperson who happens to be a woman: when, and only when, the woman is your wife, your mother, or your daughter, and there better be no tongue with those last two.

Additional time to kiss a businesswoman's cheek: when she has inexorably begun the process of kissing yours.

Warning: Do not pretend to miss her cheek and "accidentally" kiss her mouth.

Believe it or not, there are still some people who actually attempt this pathetic move—although they're not likely to remain employed for long.

When to kiss a businessperson's *hand*: when he is the pope.

Some people, notably people from southern California, believe it acceptable to refuse to shake hands with someone known to have a cold. These people are wrong.

What you do rather than refuse to shake hands: Your go ahead and shake hands, and then, shortly thereafter, you excuse yourself and wash yours.

things a man should know about **work**

Refusing to shake a proffered hand is deeply insulting and appropriate only where said hand belongs to the most odious of human creatures— we're talking KKK Imperial Wizard territory here.

When you have a cold: Tell people you're not shaking hands today because you have a cold; they will thank you, and, who knows, the practice may eventually become commonplace.

Yup, respect.

Now then: Imagine that it is 8:00 a.m., and that opportunity spreads limitless before you. Let us, friend, seize the proverbial day.

As soon as we vow never again to say, "seize the day."

chapter two

Shine the wing tips.
Dust off the Louis
Vuitton. It's the 10:00
a.m. job interview.

Perhaps we have gotten ahead of ourselves
because before one can behave appropriately on
the job, one must become employed.

**When writing to request employment:
Address your letter not Dear Sir or Dear
Madam or Personnel, but to the actual
person in charge.**

Regarding that person in charge: You check company
literature or the firm's Web site or call an assistant in her
company to verify that you've got her name and title and
address absolutely correct.

And then you put into practice these two words: spell check.

When writing to request employment: personal stationery, not the letterhead of a current or previous employer.

Especially if your current employer is Fatburger.

Your personal stationery shall be plain in aspect and lacking in such decoration as balloons and clowns.

Your résumé: laser-printed on high-quality white or off-white paper.

Qualities that this résumé paper should lack: glitter, marbling, metallic flecks, plasticity.

Do not lie on your résumé.

Exaggeration *is* lying.

Lies on your résumé can go undiscovered for decades and then, upon their sudden revelation, can get you kicked to the curb without severance.

Some companies, particularly those in the high-tech sector, prefer to receive résumés in electronic form.

While it is true that most of those high-tech companies are now shuttered and selling off their dry-erase boards for pennies on the dollar and thus are of no concern, it doesn't hurt to inquire as to the company's predilections, résumé-wise.

References: You ask someone if he's willing to vouch for you before listing him as a reference.

What to do when a prospective employer calls to ask about someone who has listed you as a reference without your permission: Recall the applicant's fondness for taxidermy, his desktop ant farm, and his garlicky homemade hummus.

things a man should know about **work**

When someone agrees to serve as a reference, send him a thank-you note and a copy of your résumé, the latter so he'll be up to speed on your doings.

Use discretion in the number of employers to whom you give your references' names, so that they are not inundated with calls about you.

Three words for when a reference is inundated with calls about you: taxidermy, ants, hummus.

When you show up for the interview: Be on time.

Definition of "on time": exactly five minutes early, no less, no more.

This definition, by the way, applies to all business appointments.

There are those who believe punctuality is the key to success—that, of course, and not soiling one's undergarments at meetings.

Punctuality is one of those things that we in the scientific community like to call a "necessary but not sufficient condition" for success.

At the interview: Wear classic business attire.

Because dressing like a Phish fan is a stupid thing to do even at a Phish *concert*, and you are not presently in attendance at a Phish concert.

More on classic business attire later.

Don't smoke in the office, nor immediately outside the office, nor within 30 minutes of approaching the office, or you will smell like a smoker—and virtually nobody likes a smoker anymore.

For that matter: Don't smoke at all, if possible, smoking having been discovered to be fatal.

Two words: breath mints.

things a man should know about **work**

When you show up for the interview: Behave perfectly and cordially from the moment you enter the reception area, and particularly be polite to the receptionist.

In re the previous: Know that most job interviewers will ask their assistant what the assistant thought of you.

And if you treated the assistant like a dung beetle, she is going to tell your prospective employer that you are an ass and an imbecile.

Don't sit down until you are directed to sit down.

You see, you want not to indicate to your prospective employers that you run the place until you are hired and, in fact, run the place.

chapter three

What are my strengths and weaknesses? Well, for starters, I have a weakness for authority figures who hold my destiny in the oily palms of their dirty little hands

When the interviewer asks for your strengths and weaknesses, the one and only weakness you cite is a weakness that you formerly had, but have since completely conquered.

Example of an appropriate weakness: excessive attention to keeping things organized, perhaps sometimes at the expense of creative thinking, which you now consider very important.

things a man should know about **work**

Weaknesses you won't be mentioning: cherry wine, cheroots, Casper the Friendly Ghost, high school gymnasts, Thai stick, pajama bottoms with footies, the fantastical mustaches on glorious display during those delicious, bourbon-soaked Tuesdays at the Ukrainian baths.

When he asks your current salary: Know that nobody, interviewers included, has any right to know your current salary.

In re the previous: You don't, of course, say it like that.

While we're on the subject of compensation secrecy: People who especially have no right to know your salary are your current coworkers whose reactions can only be resentment or pity. Tell no one.

When you learn someone's salary inadvertently, such as that time you spotted someone's paycheck on her desk and simply couldn't help reading it: Tell no one.

Especially don't tell your boss that you know what she's paying other people when you're angling for a raise. Because it will make her angry. Because she will ask where you got your information.

When a job interviewer asks your current salary: Try to divert the conversation to the salary range for this position.

If she dodges and asks again: Say something to the effect that you and your current employer have an agreement that your compensation package will be kept confidential, and isn't the issue really about how well a fit you are for this company and this spot right here and right now.

A scenario.

Interviewer: So, Johnson, what are they paying you over at Stainblot?

things a man should know about **work**

Applicant: Well, Mr. Mister, I take my salary in buffy-headed marmosets, so it's hard to translate—say, what is the salary range for this position, anyhoo?

Another scenario.

Interviewer: So, Johnson, what are they paying you over at Stainblot?

Applicant: Well, Mr. Mister, while I would be happy to provide you with my salary history at the appropriate point in our discussions, it strikes me that my current rate has little bearing on my future compensation requirements, which are $X,XXX,XXX.00—that is consistent with the range for this position, right?

The previous tactic is a bit aggressive but has among its virtues an admirably straightforward quality.

Then again, another school of thought holds that the first person to name a figure in any negotiation has already lost, because the other side may have been willing to pay more (or accept less).

In any negotiation, the first person to say "anyhoo" loses.

Finally, know this: The buffy-headed marmoset is native to Brazil and is gravely endangered and it is probably in poor professional taste to take one's compensation in imperiled jungle creatures.

Just FYI.

After the interview, if you haven't heard back: Wait one week and two days, then call to "check in."

Which reminds us—you know that gesture where you make quotation marks with your fingers as you speak certain words? Don't do that.

No, it's not a point of etiquette. It just makes you look stupid.

When you get the job: Keep your head down and your voice soft for a time, because you are fresh meat, and fresh meat is as vulnerable as a soft and fuzzy lamb.

When you're fresh meat: Keep quiet about your personal life, at least until you've figured out who is trustworthy and who is a rat.

Mr. Etiquette Man!

Question: If I'm expecting an important call, is it okay to leave my cell phone on during a meeting?

Answer: Yes. That is why Mr. Bell invented the "vibrate" mode. (If your phone does not vibrate, the answer would be no, followed by this advice: Your phone is old and should be replaced at once.)

Question: Is it okay to *answer* my cell phone in the meeting?

Answer: Yes, of *course* it's okay, because you are the one, the only, Academy Award-winning actress and America's Sweetheart, Julia Roberts! Oh—you're not Julia Roberts? You must excuse yourself and step well out of earshot to take your calls.

things a man should know about **work**

chapter four

It's sex time! When one is having sex with a woman, it is advisable to arrange the experience such that she, too, will feel as if she is having sex.

It's about her.

Except when it's about her.

Which is to say that by far the most crucially important thing to know, and to remember at all times, for the rest of your functionally pneumatic life (and afterward, too): Your primary objective is to make her very, very happy.

Because it is easy to make yourself happy. You can do that all by yourself—even with one hand tied behind your back.

Now, then: Begin at the neck.

Slowly.

And you know how when you're there, at the neck, you often make that move for the inside of her ear with your tongue? Don't do that.

Because, besides being a vector for some kind of inner-ear infection, a wet willie administered directly with the tongue is an acquired taste that very few people acquire.

See, sex is one of those tings in which everything you need to know you did not learn in kindergarten.

things a man should know about **sex**

Or in high school.

Especially not in high school.

News from the womenfolk: They want you to know that female sexuality involves regions other than the obvious naughty bits.

Further, what appeals to one woman doesn't necessarily appeal to the next.

An example, and one that might come as a shock: Some women think that too much time spent on the bazooms can become unpleasant and slightly, disturbingly Oedipal.

What appeals to no woman: premature, shall we say, resolution. Yours.

Extra Bonus Mental Picture that might assist in the avoidance of premature resolution: Dick Cheney.

things a man should know about **sex**

Also: Dick Cheney in jackboots and pasties and nothing else.

Whatever you do, don't try thinking about nuns—that just makes matters worse.

If rushing is simply unavoidable, know that you will be expected to last longer, much longer, in round two.

On the notion that good girls don't. Yes, they do.

Surefire signs that she wants to take you to bed: There are no surefire signs that she wants to take you to bed.

Good signs that she's considering it: laughs at your jokes, smiles most of the time, occasionally gently contradicts you (to show she cares enough to engage you and is confident enough to disagree), touches you softly every now and again.

things a man should know about **sex**

Handing you her panties under the table at the restaurant might mean something too.

Good signs that she's not considering it: She doesn't laugh at your jokes, doesn't smile, contradicts you too much and with vigor, shakes your hand, and leaves the building.

Appropriate euphemism for womanly bits: Snoopy.

Also: Hoosie.

Also: What's-it.

Also: Down There.

Appropriate euphemism for manly bits: Kong.

Yeah, well, it's better than Mr. Winky.

Euphemisms for sexy bits are essential because, for some unfortunate reason, the actual medical and/or scientific words for every single one of these body parts are less than musical.

And the nonmedical and/or nonscientific ones are for hunting trips more so than books.

In addition to hunting trips, blue language can also be effective when writing a *Penthouse* letter or when judiciously applied during the act (more on which later).

Never write a letter to *Penthouse*.

News from the womenfolk: You can never, ever, under any circumstances, no matter how florid or excessive you might think you sound, exaggerate the splendor of a woman's recently unclothed body.

Caveat based on further analysis of previous item: Complimenting her naked body could easily veer into a more specific analysis of same, which could present a very dangerous situation.

things a man should know about **sex**

Example: "Yeah, my jubblies are okay, but my what's-it is fat, don't you think?"

If such a situation is presented, be warned: Not only is EVERY SINGLE SOLITARY MOLECULE of her physical form absolutely perfect, including and perhaps most especially the what's-it in question, but you must be able to telegraph the idea that you really and truly believe this to be the gospel truth.

Alternative response in such a situation: Make like the wind, and blow; slip out the back, Jack; bad, bad scene.

You may be able to avoid this whole brouhaha if, before complimenting her naked body, you often compliment her clothed body.

More on the language of love. Menage à trois: French for "In your dreams."

Back-Door Action: See previous item.

Shrimping: Toe-sucking.

Felching: Do not ask.

Never use the word "intercourse."

Never use the word "coitus."

> Exception: Use of the word "coitus" is permissible if you are a professional hip-hop artist and you need something that rhymes with "annoyed us."

Never use the word "whoopee."

Because anyone who would consider using the word "whoopee," including Bob Eubanks, is probably no longer making it.

things a man should know about **sex**

Extra Bonus Mental Picture: Bob Eubanks, at one time or another in his life, has probably made whoopee.

Likewise, never use the word "lover."

Because it hasn't been 1973 since, jeez, 1973.

Likewise, never use the phrase "make love."

Because however verily you have torn off her bodice and no matter how rampant the state of your manroot, life is not a romance novel.

Use the word "manroot" whenever possible.

That was a joke.

When calling out your lover's name during sex, you want to be sure that it is your lover with whom you're having sex.

The authors of this book are permitted to use the term "lover" on occasion.

Because we are published authorities on sexuality, that's why.

The pet name Hugh Hefner employs in re his lover at any given moment: "My Special Lady."

Hef is in his 70s.

Plus: he's Hef.

Plus: The last time we checked, he had four "special ladies."

Cameras and sex: Not unless you're handsomely paid.

And handsome.

Video cameras and sex: Hey, it's your speedboat, Tommy Lee.

Speaking of speedboats: Know that sex is not a race.

Nor is it an endurance contest.

Yes, it is.

But only up to a point—her point, mostly.

On the other hand, sex can be looked at as a game, though not as a competition.

Sort of like tennis, when you're just hitting around.

Only no hitting.

If you are keeping score, and you find yourself in the lead, let her catch up.

Then, let her win.

If you win more often than you lose, then you, sir, will find yourself on the free-agent market real soon.

News from the womenfolk: It can be taken as a general article of faith that, at any given time, more than likely she is not done.

Which means you aren't either.

things a man should know about **sex**

Anything that gets her in the mood is foreplay. Even talking. Even shopping. Even, the twisted little minx, The McLaughlin Group.

Playing Barry White, while possibly effective, is a bit transparent. Likewise Roxy Music. Try middle-period Van Morrison.

Under no circumstances shall sexual congress be attempted while playing They Might Be Giants.

Plying her with two or six zombies, while possibly effective, is wrong with a capital Wrong.

Plying her atop the boss's desk: Everybody should do this at least once. Maybe. (see page 234)

It's best to go slower than you want to, especially on first and third dates.

Because on the first date too fast will make her nervous and on the third date too slow will drive her crazy. In that good way.

Now then, frequent, fleeting touches of her arm, hand, back: Yes, do that.

Some women may find your inexperience charming.

Inexperience is more charming when coupled with an earnest willingness to learn.

Her inexperience may be charming as well.

Particularly when it's coupled with one of those Catholic-schoolgirl uniforms.

Hey! Who slipped that into the book?

things a man should know about **sex**

News from the womenfolk: Many appreciate it when sex acts are preceded by acts of affection.

Women also want you to bring them a flower now and then. One flower is fine.

Women want you to leave them little love notes.

If and when you leave little love notes for women, they will leave little love notes for you.

Women want you to kiss them—really kiss them—more often than you do.

When kissing: Your eyes are closed.

When kissing: Your mouth is closed, initially.

When kissing: Your tongue should behave neither like a cold, dead, and gutted grouper lying on a fishmonger's ice block, nor should it tag at her tonsils like you're working the speed bag.

She's also disinclined to enjoy having her entire face slathered with saliva, for some reason.

Slathering elsewhere may be okay.

News from the womenfolk: They want you to hold their face in your hands during kisses.

A general principle as regards your tongue and its use with a woman—and this comes from a woman; on the woman, more so than in the woman.

The aforementioned tongue-guidance principle should be referenced in conjunction with the aforementioned ear and any of various other places that exist on your typical woman.

things a man should know about **sex**

Should you fail to heed the above advice, she will consider you sloppy and will convey that opinion to her friends and will never date you again.

And neither will her friends.

Or their friends.

Because you will be officially
tarred a Sloppy Kisser.

Sloppy Kissers are unpopular.

When it's good to hear laughter: When you're tickling someone.

When it's not good to hear laughter: Upon your disrobing.

How to remove a bra (from someone else, generally): Grasp either side of the clasp, and push the sides together, which should cause the hook to disengage from the eye.

Some guys can do this with one hand.

These are the same guys who, when faced with a frontal clasp, don't panic but quickly adjust.

If you are not one of these guys, don't fret. This is not a test of your manhood; you can ask her for help.

In fact, this is one of those activities, much like cooking and roller-skating, where ineptitude can actually appear "cute."

Alternatively, you could take one of Mommy's bras to practice on.

Um, hold it: No, you couldn't.

Wear no underwear emblazoned with boastful or otherwise humorous exhortations.

Like, say, Home of the Whopper.

Even if it is.

Which it isn't, most likely.

Unless it is, in which case, whoa.

When sex is in the offing, never wear briefs.

You should wear SOME type of underwear—just not briefs.

Because briefs are what little boys wear.

And they are not the most handsome garment.

Why briefs are not the most handsome garment: Their construction generally features support-related strapping that looks as if it were designed by the medical community, and that causes them to resemble a truss—and that's what old, feeble men wear.

Briefs are, in fact, a close cousin to the truss.

We don't know what a truss is, either, but we fear that we someday will.

You look better in boxers than you look naked.

She might look good in a g-string. You don't.

things a man should know about **sex**

If you look good naked, do it with the lights on.

As long as she, too, looks good naked.

If she looks good naked, but you don't, do it with the lights on, anyway—after hiding her corrective eyewear.

Or use candlelight.

Either way, you can't expect her to be in better shape than you.

If she is in better shape than you, consider yourself lucky, start counting the days, and be prepared for the inevitable end.

Or get thyself to the StairMaster.

Top 10 Worst Pickup Lines

10. You know, I like a girl with some meat on her.

9. Hey, can you spot me a Zovirax?

8. Here—let me wipe that for you.

7. Mmm glub glub glub heh.

6. I was thinking of going bi—but you know, with dirty pillows like yours . . .

5. Wanna touch my scar?

4. Is it just me, or are you moist too?

3. Get out of my dreams. Get into my Chevette.

2. Yo! Hey, yo!

1. I'm writing a book called Things A Man Should Know About Sex; may I ask you a few questions?

Top 10 Reasons to Turn Down a Woman's Sexual Advance

10.

9.

8.

7.

6.

5.

4.

3.

2.

1.

chapter five

We've got your workday casual—right here: Clothes do, it turns out, make the man.

Your clothes are the first thing people notice about you.

At least, they are now that you've removed that barbell piercing from your eyebrow.

As most employers do not want people to notice that their employees are Green Day enthusiasts who do a lot of faux finishing when they are not hiking Tiddlyporn Gorge, it would be best not to wear concert T-shirts, paint-stained pants, or trail boots to the office.

things a man should know about **work**

Call us traditionalists.

The nontraditionalists? You can call them, too, most likely at home, where they've been watching *Judge Judy* since their dot-com died.

Something else to keep in mind: No one ever got ignored, denied a promotion, or refused a raise because they wore a suit or sport coat to work.

The sport coat: You should accompany that with a pair of trousers, huh?

All trousers need not be khakis.

As pertains to footwear: leather and suede lace-ups and loafers.

While, strictly speaking, sandals are shoes, they are not shoes.

To those who think suits and ties and sport coats are restrictive and inhibit creative thinking: Edison didn't need Dockers to do what he did with the lightbulb. And the phonograph. And the stock ticker.

Plus: Suits and ties and sport coats are not uncomfortable. Cheap or ill-fitting suits and ties and sport coats are uncomfortable.

The Empty Suit: A useless lump who nonetheless manages to prosper at work because he always looks good.

You see, there is no shame in dressing well for work.

Dressing well for work directly translates to your eventually making more money than you otherwise would.

things a man should know about **work**

The thing is, the clothes *do* make the man.

A slight aside: The clothes that make the man often attract the woman, which, while having nothing to do with etiquette, might be something to keep in mind. Especially if you're single.

Mr. Etiquette Man!

Question: What do you wear to a "black-tie optional" event?

Answer: In our book, there should be no such thing as a "black-tie optional" event—such a designation serves only to confuse us all. Most men take it to mean they can show up in their business suit and battered wing tips, which, we suppose, they can. But that means they're guaranteeing from the beginning that they will be the least elegant men in the room, because probably more than half the attendees will wear tuxedos, and thus will look superior. So: Wear a tuxedo, or, if that feels wrong for the circumstances, an elegant black suit with a white shirt and a solid black tie—and, in any case, wear well-shined shoes.

things a man should know about **work**

If you think you must wear cologne or aftershave, you're mistaken.

Use all the mouthwash and breath mints you like.

You know that fish tie you should not wear anywhere at all, ever, no matter the circumstances (unless of course you work for Ringling Brothers)? You should particularly not wear it to work.

Put another way: How many CEOs and Nobel laureates and rising star executives have you observed wearing fish ties?

Yes, exactly our point.

chapter six

The Long March, aka Bataan via Camry, aka the commute.

Know that you are not the only person coping with the dawn of another workday mired in depression and grief—no, no, that would be everybody.

Now, then: Cheer up and quit griping if, indeed, you have a job, as it is still morning and traditionally many managers wait until the afternoon to fire people.

If you carpool, don't bring coffee.

Because other people will wish A) that they, too, had a fragrant, steaming cuppa, or B) that you were not posing such a grave threat to their upholstery, or C), and most important, that their reproductive area was not blistering from the effects of spilled scalding liquid.

All energy savings aside, you really don't want to be involved in a car pool.

To spell it out: Your weekend is dead and gone, your noggin is throbbing, and five days of head-spinning fiduciary riddles loom dead ahead—do you really want to kick off the week crammed into a Toyota full of yammering coworkers?

Similarly, urban types: The train ride to work is for reading, not talking.

Especially not talking on the cell phone.

Because the other passengers want to read *Esquire* or sleep or (bafflingly) stare blankly into dark train windows without any reading material at all, not listen to your self-important bloviating.

The other passengers probably should not be privy to the transaction of your business anyway.

And they should be even less privy to personal conversations.

Of course, we could write a whole book on cell-phone etiquette, but it all comes down to this: You know how when you hear someone nattering on their Nokia and you want to take it and stick it where its only useful function might be the vibrating answer mode? People feel that way about you, too.

What to do: Keep cell calls short.

Conduct cell calls in places where others aren't forced to listen.

And before you place each cell call, think about how you once got along fine without being in constant communication with everybody.

things a man should know about **work**

chapter seven

Life in the cubicle (and the hallway and the break room and the supply closet).

Now then: Are we all at our desks? Good. We begin.

Face time: Those hours in which your superiors and coworkers see that you are, indeed, physically at the workplace and apparently on the job.

Face time is not worth much if you have shown up late.

Calling in sick: Unless you are a person with an established and proven record of chronic ill health, calling in sick is kept to a minimum.

People who are thought to be calling in sick when they are not sick will be considered untrustworthy, whiny, and weak.

However: When you truly do have a communicable illness, you call in sick not so much to heal thyself but to spare your coworkers.

Speaking of calls: There is a right way and a wrong way to answer the telephone at the office, and the wrong way is, "Hello?"

The really, really wrong way—the kind of wrong that makes us reverse our position on cooling-off periods for firearms: scripted hellos that feature sales spiels.

things a man should know about **work**

Example: "Thank you for calling Stainblot, Inc., where protein-based fluids don't stand a chance against Spot-a-Lot! detergent. How may I direct your call?"

If re the previous, someone at every company is responsible for telling receptionists what to say when they answer the phone; if this someone is you, you have the power to stop such abuse with one memo.

If your company's phones are first answered by a voice-mail system, it is a new requirement under FCC Code 57-2231 Subsection XXIIVI that this system must immediately and at any time allow callers to reach a human operator by pressing zero.

Well, it *should* be a requirement.

The right way to answer your own phone: Simply speak your name—"Hello, Verzetti here."

The right way to answer your boss's phone: "Mr. Potemkin's office."

The way to answer your own phone when you don't want people to know they've reached your direct line: "Stainblot, Inc."

Especially if your company is not called Stainblot, Inc.

When you're calling somebody important and busy, an excellent opening line is as follows: "Is this a good time?"

Excellent response when the answer to that question is no: "I'll pop off an e-mail and try you back later."

After which time you pop off an e-mail so the important party doesn't forget you called, and then you call back later.

things a man should know about **work**

Not ten minutes later.

Three or four hours later.

When a phone conversation is the first time you've ever spoken to someone, you could probably be forgiven for saying, "Nice to meet you," because they're going to know what you mean. However, you have not actually met them.

Better to say, "It was a pleasure speaking with you."

You know those people who are nearly impossible to get off the phone, and who become so widely known as such that nobody wants to take their calls, and who, as a direct result of this inappropriate response to loneliness and desperation, suffer the actual economic damages of lost business? Don't be one of those people.

The biggest favor you can do for the previously referenced person—and for yourself: Tell them they're too difficult to get off the phone.

Why this is a favor for yourself: In future, as they hear themselves talking too much, they may learn to cut themselves off.

How to get someone off the phone: Glance at your watch and react with genuine alarm, exclaiming something along the lines of "Great horny toads—sorry to interrupt you, but I was supposed to be in a budget meeting ten minutes ago!"

(Yes, we know the person on the other end can't see you glance at your watch. Think of it as Method acting.)

And then: Thank the caller for calling, and tell her you'll be in touch.

We didn't literally mean you should say, "Great horny toads."

Everybody loves really short voice-mail messages.

things a man should know about **work**

Everybody hates really long voice-mail messages.

On your outgoing voice-mail message, you don't need to say that you can't come to the phone right now, because, well, if you could we wouldn't be listening to your outgoing voice-mail message.

Ninety-nine percent of all voice-mail messages need contain solely your name, your company name, your number, and the request for a call back.

Speakerphone? What are you, a Hollywood agent or something?

Speaking of which, babe: One does not *do* lunch. One *has* lunch. "Would you like to have lunch?" Like that.

When using a speakerphone with multiple people in the room, you must immediately inform the party you're calling that there are other people in the room.

More on telephone tech: The ubiquity of caller ID must be borne in mind before you attempt to lie about where you're calling from (especially those of you prone to calling in sick from, say, Disney World).

Or before you make crank calls to the chairman of the board.

What an assistant says when the boss is in a meeting: "I'm sorry, she's in a meeting, may I take a message?"

What an assistant says when the boss is not in a meeting but nonetheless wants to be left alone: "I'm sorry, she's in a meeting, may I take a message?"

Some people in this situation pronounce the word "message" as "massage," but fortunately not too many, and none of them is you.

Use proper grammar and clear speech—and do not attempt to eat doughnuts while talking on the phone.

Fairly or not, strong regional or foreign accents can be a hindrance to your career. You might consider a few sessions with a voice coach.

chapter eight

Some more sex! We redeem the sullied reputation of sodomy and offer suggestions on performing it. We propose the decriminalization of oral pleasuring in certain localities and consider the relative sexiness of the French, the Italians, and the British.

For our money, sodomy has gotten a bad rap.

What sodomy is, in part: sex that involves the use of the mouth.

What else sodomy is: certain types of sex that do not involve the front portion of one's partner, but that other portion.

Yes, exactly.

Sodomy of the oral variety shall hereafter be known as a Slurpee.

States that persist in criminalizing slurpees: Alabama, Arizona, Florida, Idaho, Louisiana, Massachusetts, Michigan, Minnesota, Mississippi, Missouri, North Carolina, Oklahoma, South Carolina, Texas, Utah, and Virginia.

Bumper-sticker idea, yours for the taking: "When Slurpees are illegal, only outlaws will get Slurpees."

The bumptious lawmakers of Idaho in particular seem to have a disproportionate fascination with other people's sex lives.

Evidence: In Idaho, sodomy carries a penalty of five years to life.

In fact, this little book is probably illegal in Idaho.

Research shows that jazz fans, gun owners, public-television watchers, concert attendees, and those who lack confidence in the president are among the most sexually active Americans.

Catholics are more sexually active than Protestants, but neither group is as active as Jews and agnostics.

Woody Allen is a Jewish-raised, agnostic jazz fan who attends concerts, almost certainly watches public television, and has a wife young enough to be his granddaughter.

Let us not think of Woody Allen at this time.

Self-described political liberals have more sex than moderates and conservatives.

Let's think neither of Michael Kinsley nor of George Will at this time, even though those two unlikely nebbishes would make sort of an interesting couple, no?

People who smoke and drink have twice as much sex as those who do not.

Let's think, shall we, of Elizabeth Hurley.

Speaking of drink, let's remember what a certain William Shakespeare said: "It provokes the desire, but takes away the performance."

Then again, the Bard also said: "I must dance barefoot on her wedding day, and for your love to her, lead apes in hell."

He was British.

If we may invoke Shakespeare once more, sort of: The foreplay's the thing.

Foreplay being the thing, the word "foreplay" is, of course, a misnomer.

Long before foreplay: You must meet her.

Regarding the custom of buying her a drink: You don't ask, "May I buy you a drink?"

You ask, "What are you drinking?" and then you see to it that a vessel of whatever it is she is drinking is conveyed to her.

The point at which you buy her a drink: when she's nearly but not quite finished with her current drink, and no sooner.

things a man should know about **sex**

Because to do so sooner would make it appear that you are trying to render her intoxicated.

And to do so later would be to do so too late.

And remember: Willing is better than beautiful.

Which leads us to the subject of one-night stands: Our mothers wish us to pass along their view that these are bad.

Then again, our mothers told us all cats are gray in the dark.

One-night stands: No matter how drunk you are, it is absolutely imperative that you memorize these two things before the lights go down. A: Her name. B: The color of her eyes.

Because she very well might ask you.

Do you have any idea what happens when she asks you the color of her eyes and you do not know? It is bad. Very bad.

If you don't know the color of a new Friend's eyes, for God's sake don't attempt to guess—cut your losses, plead drunkenness, admit that you forgot.

Another strategy: Tell her that her eyes are hazel or ecru or whatever and if she says, "No, they're green!" and begins sobbing, you say that hazel or ecru or whatever is a shade of green and bet her $50 that you're right.

This betting strategy does not work when it comes to her name.

So you've got to remember her name.

things a man should know about **sex**

FYI: Knowing her name or the color of her eyes becomes even more important on multiple-night stands, such as in, for example, a marriage.

After the first time: Don't call from your cell on the way home. Don't call first thing the next morning. Don't e-mail her your picture.

Do call the following evening, or the morning after that. Or not at all, you bastard.

Later in this relationship: We don't mean to disappoint you, but women may have less interest in watching porn than you do, but many of them wouldn't mind you watching it.

Should you choose to employ it in your home, call it erotica, not porn.

Despite the fact that more people are comfortable with erotica these days, it's still not prudent to keep it on the coffee table.

Who the hell are we kidding with this "erotica" crap? Porn is porn is porn is porn.

The G-spot: an interior region to which some women enjoy having special attention paid, and about which some women couldn't care less.

The G-spot: named for the German gynecologist Ernst Grafenberg.

We're thinking Ernst got his share, if you know what we mean.

How to locate the G-spot: Aim for it, and then ask her if your aim is true.

That said, if you ask every step of the way, you'll begin to remind her of her gynecologist.

things a man should know about **sex**

Which, as rewarding as a career in female reproductive medicine may sound to you, is not a good thing.

If she doesn't know or won't tell you where it is: Go straight about four inches, and aim upward, back toward yourself.

Performing oral sex when suffering from nasal congestion could conceivably result in suffocation.

Receiving it: not a problem.

The people who think they are the sexiest: The French.

The people who are the sexiest: The Italians.

The people who are the kinkiest, although you'd never guess it and they'd never confess it without being soundly tickled on their bumcakes: The British.

For people who have hangups about oral sex: Consider that human naughty bits are almost certainly cleaner than most of the doorknobs you've touched today.

Granted, one doesn't lick doorknobs, but still.

Hot and heavy date advice: Wash.

Wash there twice.

Give as good as you get.

Make that: better than you get.

News from the womenfolk: Some women appreciate the tactile pleasures of facial hair when your face is, shall we say, south of the border.

things a man should know about **sex**

News from the womenfolk: Some women do not appreciate the tactile pleasures of facial hair.

Either way, there is no sufficient excuse to grow a soul patch.

Come to think of it, always shave. Your face. And only your face.

Why you should only shave your face: A) chest shaving is practiced by affected Irish step dancers and B) shaving of any other kind of body part can be dangerous—or remarkably itchy three to five days later.

For similar scratch- and itch-related risks, sex on beaches is a flawed idea.

Also alluring but flawed: sex on airplanes, sex on 50-yard lines, sex in swimming pools, sex in old-growth redwoods (you could fall and break something that ought never break).

Average duration of intercourse among American heterosexual couples: 10 minutes.

Average frequency of sex among American heterosexual couples: seven times a month.

News from the womenfolk: Most of them are satisfied with the amount of sex in their lives.

Much more interesting news from the womenfolk: Not ALL of them are satisfied with the amount of sex in their lives.

It would not be news that most men would be willing to have more sex.

Time a couple is most likely to engage in sex: 10:34 p.m.

One in five adults has not had sex in the last year.

things a man should know about **sex**

Ten out of ten Americans lie through their pea-pickin' teeth about any and every aspect of their sexual lives.

Speaking of teeth: When good people give bad oral manipulations, it's the incisors and bicuspids that are usually to blame.

One is within one's rights to remind the administrator of one of those deals: It is an organ—not a gearshift, an organ. And a delicate organ, at that.

What to do when one discovers that a string is dangling from Down There: See The Curse.

The Curse: Some women's unfortunate term for their magical monthly cycle, about which it is necessary for you to know more than you want to know.

Number One: Never call it The Curse.

In fact, you could think of this aspect of her biological functioning as a blessing; it means she's not pregnant, which, when pregnancy is not desired, is, in fact, a blessing.

Her asking you to buy her feminine-hygiene products while you're out picking up beer is not a casual favor but a test of your manhood.

Some women feel more tender during certain days of their cycle, necessitating adjustment on your part in re her golden winnebagos and other areas.

Oral sex during this period: something you might wish to discuss together.

Meanwhile, back up north: You might think it would be great if, like the French, the Americans allowed their women to run around topless.

things a man should know about **sex**

And then you might remember that the average American weighs 40 pounds more than the average Françoise.

Viagra has allowed people who would never have been able to become porn stars to, in fact, become porn stars.

It's also allowed Bob Dole to become a TV pitchman, which totally creeps us out.

Porn stars don't have as much fun as you think they do.

Bob Dole apparently has more.

Yikes.

Younger men who don't actually need Viagra sometimes use it, too, but more for recreational purposes.

Hmmm.

Fewer than five percent of married people cheat on their spouse each year.

Sixty-seven percent of that five percent is Mick Jagger.

Our third-favorite sex joke: Woman: "Do you smoke after sex?" Man: "I don't know—I've never looked."

Percentage of men who masturbated in the past year, according to the landmark book "Sex in America:" 60.

Percentage of people who believe that figure for a second: 0.

things a man should know about **sex**

Top 10 Mood Killers

10. Saying, "Gosh, you didn't look that fat with your clothes on."

9. The sudden issuance of your girlfriend's name.

8. The sudden issuance of the word "Mommy."

7. The sudden issuance of flatulence.

6. The sudden issuance.

5. Impotence.

4. The dog copping a sniff.

3. A toddler sobbing, "Daddy, why are you hurting Mommy?!?"

2. Hearing your mother's voice on the answering machine.

1. Picking up the phone to speak with your mother.

Top 10 Bedroom Faux Pas

10. Wearing black socks.

9. Wearing pink underwear.

8. Less-than-scrupulous hygiene (exception: special-interest groups that enjoy less-than-scrupulous hygiene).

7. The biting, spanking, or inserting of anything without clearance from the tower.

6. The pushing down on the back of the head.

5. The manipulating of certain twin parts of her anatomy as one would tune a radio.

4. Covert videotaping.

3. Limiting sexual activity solely to the bedroom.

2. Excessive silence.

1. Yodeling.

things a man should know about **sex**

chapter nine

I'm mad as hell, and I'm going to salve my rage in a soothing chat with one of several thousand disinterested phone reps—yeah, that's the ticket.

Calls from angry and irrational people: What you do is you allow the aggrieved party to blow off steam, to rage and holler and fume, without taking it personally, offering soothing interjections such as "Mmm-hmm" and "I'm sorry this has been such trouble for you," and things like that.

Executives who use their secretaries to place calls for them and who won't pick up until the party they're calling is on the line—these executives look a lot less important than they think they do.

If you're on the receiving end of one of these calls: Feel no need to remain on hold for more than thirty seconds before hanging up.

Personal calls: Obviously, they're not why you're here, and thus ought be kept to a minimum.

Visits by spouse and children: best confined to brief, after-hours walk-throughs and Take Your Child to Work days, if then.

On second thought, your kid will be taking his own damned self to work all too soon—leave the rugrat at home.

When communication takes written form: 95 percent of all business correspondence begins with the words "Thank you."

Ninety-five percent of all requests you make of staffers and colleagues employs the word "Please."

things a man should know about **work**

The business letter: Current workplace mores find it just a bit too insouciant to dot the *i's* with little hearts.

The business letter: Never commit strong feelings, especially those pertaining to love and anger, to paper, especially not letterhead.

You don't want to do this with e-mail, either.

Most letters, including business letters, begin with the word "Dear," as in "Dar Mr. Jablonski."

Business letters should be as brief and to the point as possible.

Business letters that are not brief and to the point are much less likely to be effective or to spark a timely response—if only because it takes more time to craft a response to a complicated missive.

Signing off: Very truly yours, Regards, or Best.

You could try Sincerely, but, when it comes to business, you should try not to lie more often than necessary.

Brightly colored sticky notes and unusual paper clips are for teenage girls.

Sticky notes are not stationery.

Nor are e-mails.

When an e-mail suffices as a thank-you note: rarely—usually when you're thanking a close friend or family member.

things a man should know about **work**

ask
Mr. Etiquette Man!

Question: When should I send thank-you notes?

Answer: When someone interviews you for a job, takes you out for a meal or drinks, gives you a gift (even a small, crummy, corporate gift), interviews you for a magazine or newspaper, serves as a reference, a house sitter or a dog walker—in short, virtually any time that virtually anybody does virtually anything nice for you.

Question: But come on—nobody sends thank-you notes just because someone bought them a drink, do they?

Answer: You are correct, in the main. *Almost* nobody does. Those few who do, they are remembered and admired and seen as the true class acts they are.

Corporate stationery is an important element of your company's identity and should be high quality.

There is no upside to telling a coworker they look as if they've lost weight or gained weight.

On weight-related compliments: For starters, weight-loss or -gain often results from horrible illnesses you really don't want to be talking about.

On weight-related compliments: They also reveal to coworkers that you very well might have been "checking out" areas of their physical form that you have no business checking out.

Eating at your desk is to be avoided.

Because food is smelly and eating is a different thing from working and working is really the sort of thing you want your coworkers to associate with you, no?

things a man should know about **work**

When lunch must involve your desk: Move aside contracts and files and presentation graphics before you whip out the hoagie, and after said hoagie is dispatched, give the desk a good wiping-down.

Never eat anything called a "hoagie."

When lunch must involve eating at your desk: It is kindly to avoid particularly smelly food, particularly if nearby workers would be subjected to the aroma.

It is wise to avoid food that will adversely affect the character of your breath.

It is very wise to avoid food that has any externally discernible impact on your body—turning your tongue red, say, or reminding anybody of that scene from *Blazing Saddles*.

If you toss the remains of that fish taco in your own trash can, you and your colleagues will smell it the rest of the day—better to discard it upstairs in Accounting.

The previous item, while true, was a joke, and in fact contravenes the whole idea of etiquette being about—uh-huh—respect.

After lunch: The toothbrush, if possible; the mouthwash, a close second; the breath mint, at minimum.

Gum chewing: No.

Put another way, note the number of CEOs and Nobel laureates and rising star executives you have observed chewing gum on the job.

Yes, exactly our point.

Neither singing nor whistling are sounds one employs in the workplace, with the possible exception of a workplace that is a polka hall.

things a man should know about **work**

Likewise, playing a music CD on your computer is an activity best avoided.

And it doesn't have to be a Rammstein CD for people to feel that way.

To certain folks, Anne Murray can be just as upsetting as a German death-metal group.

Not a solution: headphones.

Because headphones indicate that you're more interested in hearing the Singing Sweetheart of Spring Hill, Nova Scotia, warble about snowbirds or looking at life from both sides now than you are in hearing about the boss's next project.

On the walls in many large corporations, there hang framed posters featuring photographs of landscape scenes, sometimes emblazoned with motivational exhortations, such as "Success: One customer at a time."

It is ill-advised to take a gigantic Sharpie and scrawl the profane things you'd like to do to those customers, one at a time or perhaps in groups, on these posters.

Because this is the office. You don't get to decorate it.

If, on the other hand, you are a human-resources professional and you *do* get to decorate it: Do not, under any circumstances, waste corporate resources on such condescending posters—thank you.

Metallica posters: if you're an ad-agency creative under 28 or you work for Metallica's record label.

Dilbert ephemera: That's original.

things a man should know about **work**

chapter ten

This liverwurst sandwich property of Lucine Kasbarian—do not touch!!!!!!

Everybody who drinks the office coffee should occasionally make a pot.

Notice that the previous item did not say, "All the *women* who drink the office coffee," but, rather, "everybody."

"Everybody" might include the big boss in some offices and definitely does not in others, and are you going to be the one to call him on it if he's skulking off with the last cup all day long? No. You are not.

Never leave angry public notes.

Especially never leave angry public notes concerning such trivialities as the fact that everybody who drinks the office coffee should occasionally make a pot, but, sadly, does not do so.

Instead of leaving a note: Photocopy a page from an authoritative third party, such as this very book, and affix same in the appropriate place.

Conduct the following activities not at your desk but, rather, in the washroom: hair combing, teeth brushing, makeup slathering, nail buffing, tongue scraping (shudder).

Regarding tongue maintenance: Make that your bathroom at home, preferably that one way off in the guest cabana, where we'll not have to know about it.

Don't bring papers, reports, memos, or ledgers into the men's room with you.

Why not? Well, for one thing, they're hard to wash, those ledgers.

If for some reason you have to bring papers, reports, memos, or ledgers into the men's room with you, leave them outside the stall.

On second thought, that's not an acceptable option, because someone could riffle through or steal your documents—which is to say (is there an echo in here?), don't bring papers, reports, memos, or ledgers into the men's room with you.

Upon leaving the stall, one washes one's hands. This occurs before picking up the papers, reports, memos, or ledgers.

And this occurs whether you have company in the men's room or not.

Under no circumstances should you leave the stall and announce, "Boy, oh, boy, that's the last time I order the chicken vindaloo, I can tell you that much."

Here's another idea: Do whatever it is you would do in the stall at home before you come to work.

Yes, you see, as once literally spelled out in a hit song by a certain full-figured lady of Motown fame: Respect.

You don't have to pitch in every time someone takes up a collection for a coworker's baby shower.

things a man should know about **work**

ask
Mr. Etiquette Man!

Question: What do you do when you've accidentally sent a sensitive, potentially damaging e-mail to the wrong person?

Answer: Pray with every fiber of your being that the recipient has not yet read the missive. Then, if there's any way to swing past the recipient's desk and delete the message yourself (and don't forget the Trash queue also), do so. Otherwise, you hope that the recipient has an assistant, and that the assistant has access to the recipient's e-mail password. And now: It's times like this when you truly see why it's so important to be kind to support staff, because you're going to call this assistant, and you're going to explain that you've made a terrible mistake, and that innocent people could be harmed and untold profits lost, and you're going to ask her to delete the message for you. Failing this, you've little choice but to call the recipient, lay it on the line, tell them the message was intended for someone else, and ask them to erase it. If they've seen it and found it insulting or offensive, take responsibility, apologize, and tell them you wrote the note in anger or passion. Thank-you notes would very much be in order here, as would, in some cases, a bouquet of flowers and/or the performance of hara-kiri.

You don't have to participate in the football pool.

You don't have to play "Secret Santa."

Regarding the previous office rituals, declining to participate may get you labeled as aloof.

There are worse things than being called aloof.

Among them: getting fired for neglecting your widget-selling duties in favor of baby showers, football pools, and Secret Santa preparations.

Should you find yourself accused of aloofness, open this book to this very page, hold it before your accuser, and point to the following item:

things a man should know about **work**

Nobody in this room is receiving monetary compensation to fill their lonely hours with such time-wasting frippery as baby showers, football pools, and Secret Santa extravaganzas, and, while you may choose to do so anyway, some of us have ambition and families to feed and an actual work ethic—thus, would you kindly allow me to get back to work? Thank you.

Better still: *Think* the aforementioned item without actually communicating it, and spend the five bucks it will cost to make your coworker go away. To our minds, that's five bucks well spent.

chapter eleven

It's 11:37 and we're damned pleased to meet you.

Hot on the heels of the handshake, importance-wise: the introductions.

Approaching a stranger to inquire, "I'm Joe Strummer, and you are . . . ?" is the introductory equivalent to "Who the hell are *you*?"

As a general principle, the format of the introduction should involve introducing less-important people to more-important people.

Furthermore, those introductions are phrased to reflect the fact that less-important persons should consider the introduction a privilege.

Correctly formatted introduction: Genevieve, I think you'll recognize my wife, Jennifer Lopez; Jennifer, may I present Genevieve Bouchon, my Parisian mistress?

Correctly formatted introduction: Mr. President, I'd like my daughter, Mavis Leventhal, to meet you; Mavis, this is Mr. G.W. Braintree, our nation's 43rd president.

Incorrectly formatted introduction: Mick, I'd like you to meet Schlomo Kottke, my cousin with the klezmer operation outta Philly; Schlomo, this is Mick Jagger—he's a singer, too!

Touch-call introduction: Larry King to Phyllis Diller. Or is it Phyllis Diller to Larry King?

Introducing yourself *by name*, even to people who should remember who you are, is the gentlemanly thing to do.

Because everybody, including people who shouldn't—including yourself—forgets people's names now and then.

Deliberately making others squirm for failing to remember your name is spiteful.

When you forget someone's name: Attempt to overhear them introduce themselves to others.

Failing that, when you forget someone's name: Confess immediately, apologize, and attribute your mistake to stress over your recent IRS audit and that cranial-surgery episode.

Pop quiz: What was wrong with the previous item?

Answer: You never, ever discuss in public anything to do with personal financial matters or your health (topics that are, respectively, awkward to offensive, and sad to nauseating). Instead, just confess your forgetfulness and apologize and stop. There.

If you repeatedly forget the same person's name, however, you're pretty clearly telegraphing the possibility that you find them less than crucially important.

Then again, don't feel bad: Not so many people are crucially important.

Business cards are for handing out at business functions.

Not at social functions.

Business functions: meetings, conventions, strategic luncheons, job interviews, plant visits.

Social functions: dates, church services, your daughter's school play, state dinners.

Business cards are one and three quarter inches high and three and a half inches wide, period.

They are not decorated with photos of you or drawings of animals.

On the subject of names: no nicknames.

On the subject of the prohibition of nicknames: is your workplace a fraternal organization, such as those on the campuses of larger universities, where boisterous young fellows drink beer from great plastic cups and dress as Romans? No, it is not.

On the subject of the prohibition of nicknames: That goes double for you, Mister Leader of the Free World.

(FYI: Fidel likes to be called Señor Happypants.)

Names you shouldn't use for colleagues, regardless of their junior-executive status: kid, kiddo, junior, punky, boo-boo.

Because nobody wants to be called kid, kiddo, junior, punky, or boo-boo, and seeing as how you're fully aware of your seniority and the munchkins are fully aware of your seniority, who, exactly are you trying to impress here?

Come to think, we find boo-boo kind of cute. Call us boo-boo. Thank you.

The word *cute* is used only in reference to puppies and children.

Generally, the boss is not addressed as "Boss."

"Boss" has a certain chain-gang overtone that, while perhaps applicable, may not be something your boss wants to be reminded about.

Because she's the boss.

Because she's the big-man alpha-dog 800-pound kahuna-huna hooey.

Because she wears the proverbial pants—the boogly-boogly pants!

We'll explain these pants later.

The boss is also not addressed as "Dude."

The boss is not addressed as "Dude" even if the boss likes to be addressed as "Dude"—perhaps especially so—because such behavior can only perpetuate a culture of extravagant "Dude" usage up and down the organizational chart.

The other reason the boss doesn't want you calling her nicknames: She must maintain a certain level of detachment from you so that she can fire you if necessary.

things a man should know about **work**

Calling her "Dude" will not prevent her from firing you.

Speaking of firing, dot-com refugees are to be regarded with sympathy, not derision.

Because there is nothing wrong with taking risks in the seeking of one's fortune.

Refugees of the Internet bubble are not to be referred to as "e-holes."

On second thought: The risks taken by most e-holes chiefly involved money that was not their own; plus, they called their bosses "Dude" and wore sandals to the office.

All this by way of advice to former "new-economy" e-holes trying once again to make their way in the "old economy," which it now appears is actually the only economy: Hope you were nice to people on your way up, because you're seeing them on the way down, aren't you? Yes.

chapter twelve

Lots and Lots of Sex! Exploring issues of size and flavor, the wonders of a Brazilian bikini waxing, and faking the male orgasm (Oh, yes you can!!!).

Size, we've heard, doesn't matter.

Ha!

Well, not enough to justify surgery.

Surgery: For God's sake, man, that involves knives!

Surgery also requires attending nurses, who will indulge in all manner of jokes and giggling during the procedure.

As long as we're on the subject of genital mutilation: no piercings.

Because it would hurt you, and because it would creep her out.

And if it wouldn't creep her out, that's probably because she has a carriage bolt stuck someplace where it oughtn't be.

Average size, in task-oriented mode: 11 inches.

Scared you, didn't we?

True average size, in task-oriented mode: about six inches.

On the worthiness of averages, generally: The average human has one breast and half a penis, if you get our meaning.

More important than size: fit. As in, does it?

If it does not fit, you freak bastard, you might explore options other than intercourse.

Or, perhaps, consider a larger mammal.

(It is not our place to judge you.)

Men who profess small endowment are even less trustworthy than those who boast of prodigiousness.

things a man should know about **sex**

Because anyone so fearful of prospective taunting that he's compelled to preempt it possesses a profound and potentially dangerous insecurity.

No, we are *not* obsessed with size, really, truly—this last section on the subject was no more than 50 items long.

Nonetheless, a final word: Elephant runs into a naked man on the street. Elephant looks him up and down. Elephant says: "How do you eat with that thing?"

"Blow" is just a figure of speech.

"Job," as in difficult and possibly undesirable labor, at least according to some women of our acquaintance, is decidedly not a figure of speech.

As pertains to spitting versus swallowing: Those who prefer the former—and they're well within their rights—might consider simply removing their mouths and employing a hand before this becomes an issue, so to speak.

Because spitting has distinct overtones of rejection that a hand-driven finale lacks.

In re spitting for "dietary" reasons: the caloric intake we're talking here is miniscule and would be negated with adequate exertion.

That was a joke, though you can't blame a guy for trying.

Spitting vs. swallowing, continued: it's 10 to 40 calories.

And not more than a teaspoon or so in volume.

things a man should know about **sex**

No, ladies, we do not know why a teaspoon sometimes seems like a cup.

Foods that make for a tastier oral-sex experience: pasta, potatoes, other bland items.

Foods that do not: curry, coffee, beer, spicy items.

Recipe, it then follows, for a Slurpee-free date: chicken vindaloo washed down with a Shepherd's Tit-Bitch-Dog Ale, chased with a double espresso.

For both of your information: The above tastiness rules apply equally to men and women.

Vegetarian people taste the best.

Some people say sex is like pizza—that even when it's bad, it's still pretty good.

Some people have never slept with our ex-wife.

But seriously, folks.

Bad pizza is like bad sex: It's cold, lacks spice, and if it's really bad, the crust's too thick.

We have no idea what that means.

Bikini wax: terminology for the agonizingly painful removal of hair Down There that might otherwise poke out the sides of a swimsuit.

Brazilian wax: that variety of south-of-the-border depilation that leaves only a tiny patch just above a woman's Snoopy and removes any other trace thereof, all the way back to and including the most posterior region of all.

Yes, indeed.

things a man should know about **sex**

Extra Bonus Mental Picture: Some people's sole source of employment income is derived from bodily yanking out hair from incredibly sensitive regions of women's bodies.

Sorry to stunt career exploration, but: Those professional bikini waxers are mostly women.

As for your predilections when it comes to the pilatory aspects of a new love, our advice would be: Take it as you find it.

Ostensibly, sex is free.

Oh, no, it isn't. No, free is one thing that sex most certainly is not.

You think you haven't paid for sex? Yes, you have.

Even if you haven't: You have. Or you will. One way or another.

Walking around you, day in and day out, are people so sexually liberated that they regularly participate in spouse-swapping, orgies, naked pool parties, and all manner of fantasy "play."

No, we don't know where to find these people, either.

What we do know: These people are why we have antibacterial soap.

Sometimes a woman will indicate she'd like to have sex (with you) and will disrobe and climb into bed and only then change her mind.

What you do when this happens: Accept it graciously.

When you accept it graciously, she'll feel more comfortable about seeing it through the next time.

things a man should know about **sex**

We've heard that the withholding of sexual ministrations as punishment—especially ministrations involving mouths—is practiced constantly by both men and women.

> Punishing by withholding sex should be stopped at once, but it won't be—so when it seems to be happening, discussion may be warranted.

What happens in the bedroom stays in the bedroom.

Unless, of course, it happens on top of a picnic table in the Grand Tetons, or in the lox bin at Zabar's, or atop the bar in a South Detroit pool hall, or in full-Technicolor view of God and the neighbors, in which case, well, that's where it stays.

Synonym for hickey: bruise.

> Bruises are not part of sex, unless you're Mickey Rourke.

To Mickey Rourke: Stop it.

Spanking is for misbehaving children.

Mostly.

Whips, ropes, and chains are for sex partners with Attention Deficit Disorder.

Mostly.

News from the womenfolk: Many women want you to play a little rougher than you do.

Because they told us, that's how we know.

It goes without saying that the extent of roughness must be discussed in advance.

This increased aggressiveness could manifest itself in the ripping off of clothes, the pinning down of arms, noisemaking, dirty talking, going faster and harder, tying wrists to bedposts, etc.—but again, you really want to discuss this in advance.

The biting of anything shall be discussed in advance.

When biting is desired, it should be known that the requesting party really means gentle biting and not the kind that could result in the removal of a protuberance.

It bears mentioning that the act of sex can result in child production.

Sex is better when nobody thinks pregnancy is likely.

Exception to the above: at such times when child production is the intent, of course.

Either way, the arrival of children often means that sex will happen less often and at lower volumes.

Hushed, infrequent sex has been known to make couples cross.

Solution: grandparents.

As babysitters, we mean, you sick bastard.

Sex is better when there's no risk of getting caught.

Excepting such times when sex is better BECAUSE there is the risk of getting caught.

News for the players of the field: Despite their drawbacks, as you know all too well, you must: condoms.

Ultra thin.

Condoms that are black or red or green or any other color that is not clear will make your manly bits appear to be black or red or green.

What you really want in a condom is this: glow-in-the-dark.

No, you don't.

We'd consider carefully the wisdom of purchasing hygiene-related potentially lifesaving products in the bathrooms of truck-stops.

Then again, they don't sell those French Ticklers just anywhere.

Most likely you need a standard-size condom.

A few of you may benefit from a slim fit one.

A fewer of you still may appreciate the larger-size condoms called, by the people at Trojan, Magnums.

How to tell what size you need, according to the dedicated staff at that purveyor of prophylactics, Condomania: Procure a cardboard toilet paper sleeve; achieve tumescence; insert that part of you which has achieved tumescence. If you fit in snugly, regular will do fine. If you swim around in there and bang from side to side a slim fit is best. If you don't fit at all: We salute you!

Which reminds us of a joke: Duck walks into a pharmacy and asks for a condom. The pharmacist says, "No problem. Shall I put it on your bill?"

News *for* the womenfolk: Men can fake orgasm, especially when wearing a condom.

things a man should know about **sex**

Acknowledgment to the womenfolk: It is true. Men do not fake orgasm. Men are more likely to HIDE an orgasm. We're just saying: They can.

Men should participate in all birth-control decisions.

Saying "I vote for pulling out" is not adequate participation.

What you may want, if you're in a monogamous relationship and no longer desire the apparatus for conception: a vasectomy.

Realize, players of the field: The Pill stops only pregnancy, not HIV, not herpes, not any other gnarly bedbug.

Herpes, gonorrhea, syphilis, hepatitis: All of these diseases still exist.

Herpes, gonorrhea, syphilis, hepatitis: All of these diseases still exist.

Herpes, gonorrhea, syphilis, hepatitis: All of these diseases still exist, and none of those repetitions was a misprint. You're welcome.

Once more, regarding the seriousness of this: Genital herpes is just like those painful and unsightly oral cold sores, only not on your mouth, which is to say, you don't want it.

Let us now return to happy thoughts.

The woman-on-top position allows her more control over her destiny.

Some men find the woman-on-top scenario allows them more control over their duration.

The woman-on-top position does not excuse the watching of television while she does all the work.

Phone sex, such as it is: Don't use the cordless.

Because your neighbors have baby monitors, that's why.

Computer sex: Remember that nothing really gets erased from your hard drive.

Tantric sex: a yoga-related approach that involves breathing techniques and meditation and combined energies and connection with the universe, and, allegedly, hours-long sessions featuring many orgasms.

Tantric sex is a bit contrived, to our way of thinking.

Besides, there's something to be said for rolling over and passing out.

The musician Sting once said that his Tantric prowess allows him to last five hours.

Sting is full of shit.

News from the womenfolk: There are women who do not like to receive oral affections, and who wish you'd just stop it.

Not so fast: There are many more women who wish to receive oral affections every single time they have sex.

Some women who like to receive oral sex don't always want to be simultaneously performing it.

Put another way: Some women want you to know that they consider that numerically monikered act of oral coupling overrated.

things a man should know about **sex**

One reason some women are uncomfortable receiving oral affections is their fear that men find them unpleasant Down There.

On the subject of aromas: Sexist clichés to the contrary, men and women have aromas in pretty equal measure—best get over it, say we.

On the subject of aromas: Perhaps those who don't like them just aren't cut out for sex at all, hmm?

It is perfectly acceptable to fantasize about sleeping with someone else while sleeping with the person you're actually sleeping with.

As long as that person is not, say, Dom Deluise.

Or not a person at all—a llama, for example.

Maybe it is our place to judge you, after all.

It is completely unacceptable and extraordinarily stupid to inform your partner that you're fantasizing about someone else.

In fact, many fantasies—notably those concerning furry South American fauna—are best kept to yourself.

Men and women who have been to graduate school have less sex than any other group on the educational ladder, with an average of 52 sexual acts per year.

College grads: 61 acts per year.

High school grads: 59.

Certain movements during sex, accompanied by holding the breath, can result in an inability to remember anything that occurred during intercourse for as many as 12 hours afterward.

things a man should know about **sex**

We'd like to tell you what those movements are, but we don't remember.

People who work 60 hours or more per week are ten percent more sexually active than people who work shorter hours.

About 15 percent of adults engage in half of all sexual activity.

Eighty-seven percent of that 15 percent is Bill Clinton.

When administering a massage, warm the massage oil by rubbing it between your hands before touching the recipient.

Don't leave the massage oil on the bedside table where your friends will see it.

Leaving massage oil on the bedside table where friends can see it may generate an Extra Bonus Mental Picture of you using it.

You want to be similarly discreet with the edible panties.

Ditto any other sexual appliance, particularly anything realistic.

Speaking of which, you have no idea how many women own and utilize vibrators.

Hint: lots and lots of women.

You are not to be put off by this, even if these vibrators are large and numerous.

Although it is a bit disconcerting, isn't it, that they're all so, so unflagging?

things a man should know about **sex**

Argument against getting a realistic looking sex toy: It will look as if it was removed from somebody.

If you're buying her a sex toy: Do not presume that she wants the biggest one—she does not.

Most likely.

Actually, you're smartest not to presume anything at all when it comes to her views on sex toys, and rather, the next time you're in the neighborhood of the appliance store, to ask her if she's interested in browsing.

Very few women achieve, shall we say, resolution solely as a result of, shall we say, intercourse.

Ways to up the chances: attending to that exterior special place—you know, the one that starts with C.

By the way, nobody actually eats the edible panties.

This just in: We're informed that some folks do, in fact, eat the edible panties.

Delightful with a '67 Chateau d'Yquem Sauternes, it turns out.

Persons who eat edible panties probably need a more serious self-help book than this one—or a good home-cooked meal.

The love doll: Deflate. Take to work. Inflate. Place in boss's chair. Skedaddle.

Name of the youthful Alabama attorney general who in 1999 actually, literally, seriously issued a ban on sex toys in the land of Lynyrd Skynyrd: Bill Pryor.

things a man should know about **sex**

Memo to Howard Stern: Bill Pryor's phone number is (334) 242-7401.

Number of vibrators collected for shipment to the dildo-starved citizenry of Alabama by the San Francisco-based sex-toy cooperative Good Vibrations in response to the ban: 4,000.

Number of jackasses living in Alabama: at least one.

Memo to Howard Stern: The Good Vibrations phone number is (800) 289-8423.

Some leather fetishists are so passionate about their hobby as to refer to themselves in the aggregate as the "leather community."

Never use the words "leather community."

Dressing up as policemen, nurses, schoolmarms, presidents, Kentucky colonels, telephone linemen, pizza delivery boys, whatever: Knock yourself out, so long as we don't have to see it.

Sex three times a week can burn off 7,500 calories a year, the equivalent of 75 miles of running.

This does not mean that you can skip the gym.

The more sex you have, the less likely you are to suffer heart disease.

Also, the more garlic you eat, the less likely you are to suffer heart disease.

Unfortunately, the more garlic you eat, the less likely you are to have sex.

things a man should know about **sex**

Top 10 Euphemisms for Sexual Intercourse

10. Interior decorating.

9. Parallel parking.

8. Ugandan discussions.

7. Get up in the hat rack.

6. Throw a leg over.

5. Do a bit of front-door work.

4. Let Jack in the orchard.

3. Put Barney in the VCR.

2. Take a turn among the parsley.

1. Lead the llama to the lift shaft.

Top 10 Favorite Sex Acts for Men

10. Receiving oral sex.

9. Receiving oral sex.

7. Receiving oral sex.

6. Receiving oral sex.

5. Receiving oral sex.

4. Receiving oral sex.

3. Receiving oral sex.

2. Receiving oral sex.

1. Receiving oral sex.

things a man should know about **sex**

chapter thirteen

Your gal Friday, who, chances are better than fifty-fifty, might prefer not to be called a "gal."

Being that one of the chief secrets of a successful career is to make the support staff love you: Always greet your gal Friday with a smile and a genuine good morning.

On the use of the term "gal Friday": only as a humor device, and only if it can be convincingly demonstrated later in a harassment lawsuit that all sides understood the humor.

Which is to say, in most cases, the use of terms like "gal Friday" is not a good program.

In fact, neither gender is especially well served by the use of such terms as "Babe" or "Honey" or "Sweet Peachy Bottom," and those who employ them should be instructed to instead use people's actual names.

More important than an MBA: an understanding of the importance of assistants as sources of intelligence and know-how, and how to make them happy.

How to make assistants happy, step one: Notice that they exist.

An aside: The aforementioned rule applies to human beings in general.

How to make assistants happy, step two: Having noticed their existence, recognize that their worth as human beings is exactly equal to your own, even possibly greater, and speak to them in tones that convey friendliness and respect.

things a man should know about **work**

How to make assistants happy, part three: While not mandatory, the occasional modest gift or help with a heavy parcel or definitely nonsexual compliment on clothing does not hurt.

Caveat: Establish dominance quickly.

Because you don't want to find yourself in a situation like Drew Carey and that woman with the makeup.

Limit the number of drinks you consume and the amount of time you spend with employees below your station.

The aforementioned does *not* mean it is acceptable to be unkind to or look down upon employees who rank lower than you do; it is a part of the professional detachment you must preserve, just as your boss does over you, in the case of needing to discipline someone.

It's about order and discipline and limits—all of which allow an office to function more smoothly than one in which the assistants call their bosses "Dude-sicle"—such as in the Army, where the officers have their own mess and their own nightclub, you see.

> People who are rude to support staff receive the attendant dislike of support staff—and then, when the chips are down, they discover how badly they need the support staff.

Regarding your secretary: Don't call him your secretary.

Also don't call him "boy."

Though if he is a female, it might be amusing to call your secretary "boy."

If possible, see to it that your secretary receives a new title along the lines of "administrative assistant" or "personal assistant" or "department coordinator" or "assistant to the King," where the King is you, or some such.

things a man should know about **work**

Personal errands: The extent to which your assistant should be running personal errands for you depends on many factors, among them his expertise and experience, your seniority, but, most important, the agreed-upon responsibilities his position entails.

For example, the executive aide to the CEO of Sony does not run out for sandwiches; she phones up a lesser secretary or messenger who then runs out for sandwiches.

The assistant to Bob, the manager of Coconuts Records and Tapes at Olde Orchard Centre, might reasonably be expected to procure Bob's Subway Club.

When it is okay to expect your secretary to pick up your dry cleaning: when your secretary was hired with the understanding that he would now and then pick up your dry cleaning.

Or when you ask really nicely and he agrees without hesitation.

Regarding sex with an assistant: so long as it is somebody else's assistant.

From a different firm.

In another city.

When you are called upon to help an unimpressive underling find work elsewhere via a recommendation you'd rather not provide, it is better to say you don't know enough about the person than it is to trash them.

Which, by the way, is the same thing as trashing them, only it's not "actionable."

Which isn't to say you should praise without reserve someone you do like: Your reputation, in such cases, is affected by their behavior once they get the job.

How to give a recommendation: Make a brief list of the person's positive attributes and recite that list over the telephone.

After twelve months in your employ, your assistant will know more about you than you know about yourself.

This can make her either excellent counsel or your worst enemy. Which is up to you.

It is, once again, a matter of respect.

How she can be your worst enemy: She can unveil your shadings of the truth, disseminate your bad-mouthing, and lay bare your practice of filching Post-Its and paper clips for home use.

Mr. Etiquette Man!

Question: When I'm using a speakerphone, is it necessary to tell the person I'm calling that there are other people in the room?

Answer: It is absolutely necessary, unless you are conducting hostage negotiations or if you want the boss to discover that his staff calls him "Orca." You should also know this: When you're on a speakerphone, your every cough, burp, keystroke and rustling comic-book page is amplified and duly noted on the other end of the line.

In the office, there should be no shadings of the truth.

Except, of course, for the obviously necessary types of truth-shading.

There should be no bad-mouthing.

There should be no gossiping.

Put another way: How many CEOs and Nobel laureates and rising star executives have you observed whispering about which manager is shtupping whom?

Yes, exactly our point.

True, this sharing is something we humans like to do. It can make life easier, make us feel better about ourselves, make us tingle with the fresh joy of discovery. No one disputes that. It is just inadvisable if you wish to remain comfortably employed.

One other thing, above all, that there should not be: hanky-panky with your gal Friday.

Why? Hoo-boy!

As pertains to other staff: The same rules of conduct that apply to your G.F. should apply to them. And also this:

Listen.

Understand.

Encourage.

Inspire.

Allow them a certain amount of autonomy in their jobs.

Praise them when they do well.

things a man should know about **work**

If you are a manager of people, it is essential to bestow a certain amount of praise upon those people, or they will eventually shoot themselves—or you.

When you're about to be shot, etiquette dictates that you throw up your hands, scream like a Canadian figure skater, and run like hell.

Wetting your pants is an acceptable option, but by no means necessary.

Back to your staff: Gently discipline them when they do ill.

When we speak of discipline, we don't mean the kind administered by an English schoolmistress in horn-rimmed glasses and knickers.

Sadly.

Discipline should take place privately.

Discipline should proceed on the presumption that Sully, say, has made a small error and because he is a good and smart man—would you have hired him if he were not?—you both understand that he will make no future small errors.

Also, listen to his response to your concern. He may have a good excuse.

Generally, excuses are like opinions: Everyone has one and most are wrong. Still, it doesn't hurt to hear it.

Discipline is best delivered with a bedrock of praise.

See, the idea is to create an environment for your subordinates that you, if you were a subordinate, would like to work within every day for the next thirty years.

Hit it, Aretha: R-e-s-p-e-c-t.

things a man should know about **work**

chapter fourteen

The three-Pellegrino lunch.

A lunch meeting is an appointment, and an appointment is a time-related event to which one is not late.

Period.

Also, one is not too early.

The reason you don't want to be early: When the rest of your party arrives, you'll look like somebody with time on his hands—and therefore with less authority and responsibility than the rest of your party.

You'll also feel sorry for yourself, sitting there forlornly, twirling an empty wineglass, trying not to feel jilted.

What to be: on time.

If you are late—if, say, your cab has been caught behind the circus parade—call the restaurant and ask them to let your dining companions know.

Yes, this is one of the few appropriate uses for a cell phone, after which you will put it away and not use it again until after the lunch.

Away means turned off and lodged securely in your pocket or bag, and not on the table where you might be tempted to spin it round and round.

things a man should know about **work**

Whoever proposed the lunch pays for the lunch.

The previous item holds true regardless of either party's age, rank, or gender.

When proposing a lunch or dinner, determine from the outset whether any guests have complicated diets or intense political leanings as regard food, and select the restaurant accordingly.

That does not mean you take Serbians to the Croatian Café, or that you take vegans to Sizzler, although that sounds like a tickle. What it means is exactly the opposite of that, smartypants.

It is a warm gesture to take foreign visitors to a place that serves food they'll appreciate and understand—a place that serves the cuisine of their homeland, perhaps.

It's often a good idea to select a restaurant where the staff knows you and where your connectedness might impress your guests. Just don't be overbearing or showy about it.

If circumstances make it too difficult to ascertain personal culinary data: Select a restaurant that's not exotic or controversial (with Americans, you can't go wrong with Italian) and that features a widely varied menu.

But watch that splattery spaghetti.

Also: You could ask your guests beforehand what sorts of food they'd like. They might have a powerful hankering for fried chicken.

Traditionally, you don't talk business until dessert and coffee.

What you talk about before dessert: families, hobbies, sports, people's houses, hometowns, career trajectories, upcoming vacations—in short, the same things you talk about when getting to know anybody personally.

What you don't talk about: your health, your SugarBusters diet, your debt, your politics, faith-based anything, the Middle East, how bad the food is, your boss's hot wife.

things a man should know about **work**

Your napkin goes into your lap the moment you sit down.

When you get up to take a phone call or to use the bathroom, you leave your napkin on your chair, not on the table.

Because no one wants to see your wrinkled, stained linen next to his swordfish carpaccio.

Mr. Etiquette Man!

Question: What does fine wine service look like?

Answer: a) The sommelier shows the bottle to the host to confirm that she's getting the wine she asked for. The sommelier uncorks the bottle and hands the cork to the host, who inspects the cork for dryness or crumbling and verifies that the cork is imprinted with the correct château or brand. Many people sniff the cork, but not you, because you know that there is nothing you can learn from sniffing the cork that you can't learn better from sniffing the wine. Plus, it looks stupid.

b) The sommelier pours a small amount into the glass of the host, who smells it (without an audible inhale) and tastes it with a minimum of fuss and bother (and certainly no gurgling), and nods her approval.

c) If the host disapproves—that is, if she believes the wine has gone bad because of improper storage or a faulty cork (the wine is "corked")— she should quietly mention this problem to the sommelier, who must also taste the wine to see if he agrees. If he does, the bottle will be replaced without charge.

d) The host knows better than to reject a bottle of wine if she doesn't know what she's talking about.

Note to those waiters who snap up napkins from chairs, refold them, and place them back on the table: Don't. Again, leave it on the chair.

Feel free to have a glass of wine at a business lunch, particularly if others at the table are doing so.

Do not feel free to have a second glass of wine.

Regarding the wine: Don't talk about it.

Even if you're the consummate authority on Sauternes. Especially so, in fact.

What to do when someone asks you to select the wine and you're *not* the consummate authority on Sauternes: Discreetly signal your waiter, tell him what people have ordered, and ask for his recommendation.

What to do when the waiter asks for your price range, wine-wise: Point to an entry on the wine list.

Wineglasses are shaped the way they are shaped in order to best concentrate the aromas beneath your nose.

The miniature wineglass is for cordials, sherry, or dessert wine.

You really needn't worry about the glasses. That's what waiters are for.

When it comes to the food, never order anything that is difficult to eat.

Because nobody wants to shake a greasy hand.

Because the contract isn't going to the guy who's licking hollandaise off his tie.

Because slurping spaghettini out your nose is unlikely to get you a raise.

(Admittedly, there may be some lines of work in which the ability to slurp spaghettini out one's nose might get one a raise.)

Mr. Etiquette Man!

Question: How do I ask for a raise?

Answer: First, consider honestly whether you truly deserve one. No—*honestly*, we said. It doesn't matter that you want more money; most people do. It doesn't matter much that coworkers are making more than you are; that generally means that your boss considers them more valuable or experienced (although it might just mean they are "squeakier wheels"—that is, that they've gone to the trouble to ask for more money). Now then: Go in with evidence (no charts, no graphs, but a few firm figures in your head). Talk of recent accomplishments, awards you've won, increases in your responsibility, increases in the number of employees you oversee or clients you maintain or widgets you have sold. Stay positive and friendly. Speak of your desire to grow with the organization. Then, when the big guy comes across with a handsome boost, write him a thank-you note and forward an appropriate cut to the authors of this book, care of our publishers. Fifteen percent would do nicely. Thank you.

Foods to avoid at a business luncheon: hollandaise, French onion soup, barbecued ribs, salads of unchopped greens in splatter-prone vinaigrette, anything you would hold in your hands and bite pieces from, anything involving hundreds of tiny bones, anything involving copious amounts of brightly colored sauce.

Speaking of copious amounts, a business lunch is not the place to demonstrate how much you can pack down your gullet.

When you bite down on a piece of gristle: Discreetly take in a deep breath, so as to attract as little attention as possible, and, having used your tongue to more the gristle to the front of your mouth, just behind the lips, expel it with a sharp burst of air toward the best-looking woman at the table. Then, look surprised.

The authors of this book are completely at a loss as to the presence of the previous entry.

Here's how it's really done: When you bite down on a piece of gristle, lift your napkin or spoon to your lips as if preparing to dab or take a sip of soup, and, all the while acting natural so as not to draw attention, convey the item down to the rim of your plate.

The cutlery placed horizontally above your plate—that is, where the twelve would be if your plate were a clock—that cutlery is for dessert.

The small fork is for salad, unless it's a funny-looking small fork, in which case it's for extracting seafood from its shell (which you shouldn't be doing anyway, per earlier advice, because of the splatter problem).

Similarly, the funny-looking knife, should there be one, is for fish.

things a man should know about **work**

The small knife is for bread.

The big spoon is for soup.

Not the big spoon that's in the whipped parsnips—that's for serving the whipped parsnips.

All you really need to know about which fork goes where: The cutlery you should be using for each course will be the cutlery farthest from either side of the plate during that course.

Scientific fact: Nobody is paying the slightest attention to which fork you're using, unless you've stuck it into your head.

In the rare instance that someone is paying attention, they are thinking one of two things: a) that they, themselves, are using the wrong fork, or b) that you are from Europe.

If they should ask: You "attended university" in Vienna, where you also learned a thing or two about how to slice a living man's skin from his musculature with a grapefruit spoon, and boy oh boy, don't you wish people would stop watching you eat your vichyssoise.

Whoa, sorry about that, but it does remind us that it's impolite to stare, even at people who eat funny.

Speaking of Europeans, and most of the non-American world: The fork stays in the left hand at all times, and the knife in the right.

The above is known as the Continental style of eating, and it is more logical and efficient than the American style, in which the fork is switched to the right hand for every bite.

Not that you can't eat that way if you want, Cletus.

things a man should know about **work**

You order dessert if your host orders dessert.

If you are the host, ask if your guest would like dessert, and act as if you mean it.

To signal to a waiter that you're not finished eating but are merely taking a break for a moment: Place knife and fork as if they are the hands of a clock and it is 4:40.

To signal to a waiter that you're done with a course: Place knife and fork on the plate, parallel to one another, as if it is 4:20.

Warning: These signals won't work at TGI Friday's.

Check grabbing is just as unattractive in a business context as in a personal one.

Worse: intentionally slow, faux check-grabbing, just in time to fail to attain it.

A pair of suggestions that should take care of this check business: a) You're picking up the check? Oh, thank you; b) Here, let me get this.

If your companion gets the check, you dip into your pocket for the coat-check person.

The Hollywood three-way: You have a business lunch, you split the check, you seek your company's reimbursement for the entire bill, then you write it off on your personal income tax return.

You might want to avoid suggesting the Hollywood three-way at certain sensitive business lunches, such as those at which your future employment is under discussion, or when you're dining with clergy.

Or with your in-laws.

Guidelines for a business dinner: Apply the guidelines for a business lunch, only, you know, later in the day.

Also: At dinner, you might allow yourself that second glass of vino.

We said second, not twelfth.

Mr. Etiquette Man!

Question: What are the rules of proposing a toast?

Answer: An important and delicate art, that of the toastmaster, and one that can immeasurably enhance an event—and your reputation. A few notes: The host of the affair is the first to make any toasts, which are generally directed to the guest of honor. (If you are not the host, you must seek permission before clanging your spoon against your glass. Also, be very careful clanging glassware—if you break it and soak the table, you'll receive more attention than you wanted.) Toasts may occur at the beginning, midpoint, or end of a meal. At a stand-up reception, aim for the middle of the event, when the most people are likely to be present. First, see to it that nobody's glass is empty, whether they're drinking wine, water, or Cherry Coke. Be sure that you are not drunk. Request everyone's attention (if it's more than a dozen or so people, do so in a standing position), and present your remarks within five minutes, preferably within one. Upon completion, make eye contact with the honoree, raise your glass, and say, "To Bob." If you are on the receiving end of a toast, you don't sip your drink with the rest of the table; you sit there with your hands in your lap. Afterwards, you offer a return toast—a very, very brief one—thanking the host for the hospitality. *Skol. Slainte. Salud.* Cheers.

chapter fifteen

The two o'clock meeting (ha—made you yawn).

In addition to having a prearranged starting time, meetings should have a prearranged ending time.

The two o'clock meeting should never have been scheduled for two o'clock, because everybody will be sleepy after all that vichyssoise.

Unless you believe there's a scarcity in the number of people who hate you, do not schedule meetings cruelly, such as the Friday afternoon of a holiday weekend.

Schedule meetings in the morning, but not too early, and as far in advance as is feasible.

The boss gets the comfy chair at the end of the table farthest from the door.

In fact, the boss *always* gets the most comfortable chair.

Because she's the boss.

Because she's the big-man alpha-dog 800-pound kahuna-huna hooey.

Because of—you guessed it— those gosh-darn boogly-boogly pants!

things a man should know about **work**

Of course we have not been drinking. Why do you ask?

Wait until you are instructed to sit, because the boss may have designs on the seating arrangements.

You know that joke, where the junior manager facetiously says, "I supposed you're all wondering why I've gathered you here today"? That's been done.

Meetings should begin even when some invitees are late—it will then be their responsibility to get caught up on what they missed.

It is generally inappropriate for the boss to publicly humiliate people by calling attention to them when they're late to a meeting.

Whether you're running the meeting or merely participating in it, it should be everybody's Job One to a) stay on the subject and b) keep it moving.

What this means: Do not use a staff meeting to push your own parochial agenda.

Way to keep a meeting moving: Confine your input to issues that truly relate to everyone at the table, and reserve more special-interest issues for small-group discussion.

Another way: Offer to put your ideas on paper and circulate them later.

Yet another: Suggest that other meeting participants put their ideas on paper and circulate them later.

Re the previous item: This technique cannot be used on your boss, no matter how egregiously she may be blathering.

things a man should know about **work**

Correct! Once again you must defer to those boogly-boogly pants.

It helps, of course, to remember that it is never worse to be late for work than on the day of the morning meeting, when your embarrassment is magnified and publicly displayed for the schadenfreude of all your enemies.

Schadenfreude: The word coined by the Germans for taking pleasure in the misfortunes of other people.

Don't throw around foreign words assuming that others will understand them.

Plus, don't go feeling schadenfreude, anyway, because the world is a fair and just place where either karma or dogma or the afterlife will see to it that eventually everybody gets what's coming to them.

Yeah, right.

Feel free to gloat; just do so quietly and to yourself.

And when in Frankfurt for meetings, don't persist in bringing up that World War II business.

On meetings: It is important that you demonstrate your value by contributing to the discussion.

Your contribution does not start with putting your foot on the conference table.

If you happen to be the boss: You know, of course, to invite to meetings only those people who truly need to be there.

On meetings: Circulate an agenda in advance.

Regarding that agenda: Stick to it.

things a man should know about **work**

You know that prearranged ending time for the meeting? That is when the meeting should end.

Regarding meetings at other companies' offices: You don't sit down until someone tells you where to sit down.

And when you're told where to sit, you sit there, feet on the floor (not on the table), arms comfortably in front of you (not laced behind your neck), and your head comfortably erect on your shoulders (not supine on your notebook), no matter how tired or comfortable or madcap you want to be.

At meeting's end, it is also helpful to recap the decisions made at the meeting, so everyone has appropriate marching orders.

What happens at the convention stays at the convention, particularly when what happens has something to do with your boss's inappropriate behavior.

Because she's the boss.

Because she's the big-man alpha-dog 800-pound kahuna-huna hooey.

Because she wears those famous pants.

Speaking of out-of-town behavior, despite the fact that the hotel bill does not explicitly state whether your pay-per-view selections featured pornography, nobody back at the office is going to think you watched *Chicken Run*.

chapter sixteen

Got time for a quickie? The exercise that will improve sexual performance, the perils of prematurity and rough sex, and the relative merits of the crab, the rabbit, the wheelbarrow, and the Cooper.

When she says she loves your love handles, she means it.

When she says she loves your little tummy, she means it.

When she says she loves your sunken chest: Nope.

Lesbians have more sex, and longer episodes of sex, than anybody else.

Unfortunately, lesbians do not wish to have sex with you.

The Persians used to say: a woman for procreation, a young boy for pleasure, a melon for ecstasy.

You are not to follow the advice of those Persians.

Although there's certainly no harm in the occasional violation of a melon.

Our second-favorite sex joke: Man: "Do you like Kipling?" Woman: "I don't know, you naughty boy—I've never kippled."

things a man should know about **sex**

The Chinese believe that a man derives good luck by carrying a pair of women's underwear on his person, and a woman by carrying a pair of men's.

Nowhere does this Chinese luck policy specify that the underwear needs to be *worn*.

There is an exercise that both men and women can perform to improve their sexual performance, and this exercise is called the Kegel exercise.

The Kegel exercise: repeatedly clenching the pubococcygeal muscle, better known as the muscle one tightens to stop oneself from urinating.

In men: Kegels have been shown to produce greater control over timing at the finish line, and also to improve one's ability to make one's willie dance up and down to the delight of any and all onlookers.

In women: Kegels have been shown to strengthen certain interior muscles that produce those earthshaking, mind-blowing you-know-whats—and that also gives one more control over internal squeezing/tightening motions.

One more reason to date the women of the Olympic equestrian team: The Kegel exercise happens naturally to people who ride horses.

When the moment strikes: It is not only unnecessary but actually kind of inappropriate to repeatedly holler "God!" (What are you doing, there, anyway, thanking the supreme being for this long-sought slice of sizzling action?)

However, it is better to yell "God?" than it is to yell, say, "Mommy!"

things a man should know about **sex**

Other words best avoided during one's exertions: Pretty Mama, Hot Papa, darling daughter, cousin, auntie, grandma, Principal Skinner, Senator Kennedy, Dr. Albright, and Borgnine, you virile hunk of man, you.

Regarding threesomes: They make better fodder for naughty movies than a Saturday night out (or in, as the case may be).

Should you be so lucky threesome-wise—and don't hold your breath—everyone needs to get equal attention.

Then again, you may not want the equal attention rule to apply if it's you and another guy occupying the two-thirds majority of this particular congress.

This just in: In most cultures, high-fiving one's buddy over a woman's shoulder as one approaches, shall we say, resolution in a threesome, is considered, at a minimum, indelicate.

A sly, simple "Duuuude!" will suffice.

Jokes, folks, is what those two previous entries were, we'll thank you to realize.

We know that you give some of your best performances before breakfast, but let's everybody brush our teeth first.

Some women consider it rude for men to begin sleeping immediately after sex.

Whether they're right or wrong on this point, it's not as if cuddling is strenuous, now is it?

News from the womenfolk: Some ladies would just as soon crack a beer and turn on Speedvision as they would get all snugglykins after the fireworks.

things a man should know about **sex**

If she rolls over and begins to snore, don't chase her for aforementioned snugglykins.

Unless you are a published authority on the subject of sexuality, you are not to use the word "snugglykins." News from the womenfolk: The vast majority of women do *not* prefer cuddling to sex. They prefer sex.

On condoms: At the completion of one's exertions, one does not hold up the condom to inspect it.

Nor does one stretch it between thumbs and fingers like a rubber band so as to shoot it into the wastebasket.

Rather, one drops said condom discreetly onto the floor, close enough to the bed that it doesn't become a pedestrian hazard, where it can be retrieved and disposed of after an appropriate period of snugglykins.

News from the womenfolk: Responsibility for retrieving and disposing of said prophylactic the following morning falls to—better believe it—you.

Mirrors go on walls.

Not on all four walls, please.

Beds are not round, vibrating, canopied, or filled with water.

Sheets are not satin, polyester, floral, or visibly besmirched.

Regarding sex in cars: Bear in mind the car scene from *The World According to Garp*.

things a man should know about **sex**

Percentage of men who have received physical affection Down There from another's mouth: 79.

What we want to know is this: Who IS this sad, sorry, woebegone 21 percent, and could someone please give them a hug?

She can say no to sexual relations.

You cannot.

For many reasons, but especially because you don't want to give her the ammunition to say no the next time you want her to say yes, because you one time said no.

Speaking of which: No means no.

Except when it means yes, and it almost never means yes.

When it means yes: during consensual sexual roleplay of the mild S&M variety.

Sexual roleplay in which no means yes requires the selection of another word—a safe-word—that actually means no.

We like the word "Rumplestiltskin."

Also: "Bhoutros Bhoutros Ghali."

It's okay to lie about certain aspects of your sexual history.

Not aspects that involve viruses or her sister.

Because the truth will out, eventually, and when it does—hoo, boy!

things a man should know about **sex**

Contrary to persistent reportage touted on the covers of certain women's magazines, there are no "new" positions.

So relax. You pretty much know them all.

There is no shame in the missionary position.

That said, exclusive deployment of the missionary: Snoresville.

The missionary position was named for spreaders of the gospel who preached that men should assume a dominant posture over women in all endeavors.

While we're tempted to say, "Spread this gospel, baby!," we shan't.

Not again, anyway.

If you're reading this, you're probably not a missionary.

Whether or not you are a missionary, you're a blame fool to eschew the carnal pleasures of the crab, the snake, and the wheelbarrow.

The crab: Man lies on his back, woman sits atop him facing away from his face; upon insertion, she leans back and looks up at the ceiling, supporting herself with her hands and feet on the floor.

The snake: Either man or woman lies on back, other lies on top, with bodies fully in contact from toes to faces, and insertion occurs with no spreading of the legs at all. Sssssssuper.

The wheelbarrow: Man is standing; woman is on floor in front of him, her body facing down. He hoists her by the legs and hips, she lifts her torso with her arms, as if aiming to perform a handstand, and, insertion! Can be utilized to parade around the house or garden during the act.

things a man should know about **sex**

Extra Bonus Position: The Cooper, in which you lean back dispiritedly with beads of sweat on brow, while she repeats over and over, "Don't worry, it happens to everyone—let's just cuddle."

It is crucially important that you do not have sex the same way every time.

Put another way: Having sex the same way every time makes people want to have sex with different people just to vary things.

News from the womenfolk: They would appreciate it if you would indulge their occasional desire to integrate things like bubble baths and scented candles into the making of the love.

Caveat: Sex in bathtubs is not so easy. But then nothing worth doing is.

News from the womenfolk: It is not totally inconceivable, this idea of asking her to face the wall—but you first must know her very, very, very well.

If you do not know to what the previous item refers, it is best that it stays that way.

things a man should know about **sex**

Top 10 Worst Morning-After Exit Lines

10. Is it just me, or do you feel a burning sensation?

9. Hey, you're not Mary Ann!

8. Hate to go, but it's my sister Peggy Sue's due date and Momma said I'm not allowed to miss the birth of one more kid of mine.

7. If you need to reach me, I'll be at the rectory.

6. Grab the trash on your way out, 'kay, babe?

5. Can you leave me a few of those condoms?

4. Damn! Left the puppies in the dryer!

3. So what do I owe you?

2. You're 18, right?

1. Whoa, that was a mistake.

Top 10 Worst Breakup Lines

10. I think we both know this isn't working out.

9. I think one of us knows this isn't working out.

8. If I've told you once, I've told you ten times: The name is Jennifer now!

7. I'm trouble, baby, with a capital T.

6. You're a real ballbuster, you know that?

5. My wife is having a bigger problem with us dating than I thought she would.

4. We'll always have Coney Island.

3. It's not you, it's me.

2. It's not me, it's you.

1. Buh-bye.

things a man should know about **sex**

chapter seventeen

Courtesies and niceties inside and outside the office, including door holding and what to do about people who don't smell right.

Regarding holding doors open for women: Forget any admonitions to the contrary and just do it.

Because women love it.

Because men love doing it.

Here's the thing: When the circumstance warrants, you also hold doors open for men.

When the circumstance warrants: when you have reached a doorway first and someone is close behind.

Because door holding is no longer about gender niceties—it's about courtesy and deference regardless of who's carrying the Y chromosome.

Because in these times of scarcity, chivalry-wise, such a glimmer of civility and kindness and class brings forth wellsprings of appreciation from either sex—and your actions will be remembered by all who witness.

If a woman should, say, sneer at you for performing such a kindly gesture, feel sorry for her.

Also hold doors for visiting dignitaries and superior officers in your organization, allowing them to precede you.

things a man should know about **work**

Similarly, opening the passenger-side car door for your guests before getting into the car yourself is a pleasant and courtly gesture.

You know, come to think of it, your wife might appreciate it, too. And you know, the longer you've been married, the more she'll appreciate it.

It's called respect.

The concept of door holding extends also to elevators, particularly when some poor soul is dashing madly to make it onto yours.

Here's a good one: You stand in the elevator and smile blankly at the person rushing toward you, feinting at pushing the "close" button to tease them.

Okay, it's not *that* good.

The person closest to the exit of the elevator is the first to exit, regardless of gender—a policy best observed in other tight spaces, too, such as tight crevices in caves and narrow tunnels beneath foreign embassies.

If a man and a woman are alone in an elevator, no harm should come to the man who, with a subtle, elegant gesture, invites the woman to exit first.

When holding doors for people, do not do so with a showy, exaggerated flourish. Do not, for example, doff your hat and bow. Just do it in a matter-of-fact way, without calling excessive attention to yourself or your kindly actions.

Speaking of which, as a general principle, there is never a need to doff your hat and bow.

Times not to hold doors open for people: when you're part of a large crowd of strangers surging into a public building, a train depot, say, in which case it shall be first-come, first-through.

things a man should know about **work**

One need not carry chivalry to such an extreme as to toss one's coat onto a puddle to protect a lady's shoes—madness, that.

But it is nice to rise from your seat when she arrives at or leaves a table.

You can do this for men, too—not when they effect a temporary exit, to the loo, say, but when they're departing the premises.

Sure, it's a little bit of work, but do it and do so effortlessly and you'll think you're in one of those romantic comedies from the thirties and forties, which, as guides for behavior, rank far above, say, *Porky's*.

No longer necessary and a bit excessive: lighting a woman's every cigarette, particularly since nobody smokes anymore.

What to do when you notice that someone's trousers are unzipped: You affect a Boston accent and loudly hiss, "The bahn door is open at McGillicuddy's fahm!"

That was a joke—particularly the Boston part—and one that even we, its authors, don't fully understand.

You tell this someone quietly and matter-of-factly, "Someone, it looks as if your pants have come unzipped."

Why you do this: because you, too, may someday notice at 5:00 p.m. that McGillicuddy's got a situation down there and that you wore the pink satin boxers and that this unhappy condition has probably existed for hours and hours, including straight through that meeting with the Dutch financiers, seeing as how you haven't used the can since 9:30, and because if a friend had just noticed and spoken up, all this misery could have been prevented.

What you do when you notice that someone has bits of food stuck between his teeth: Presuming he's someone you like and for whom you have esteem, you pull him aside and tell him, "Marty, you might want to check the mirror, because I think there's something stuck in your teeth."

When it's not someone for whom you have esteem: Indulge in a moment of schadenfreude, chuckling softly to yourself.

Trickier still—what to do when a coworker has overwhelming body odor: "Cooper, this is rather awkward, but I hope you'd do the same for me. You might want to try a stronger antiperspirant, maybe one of those new brands designed for active people like yourself."

What to do then: Duck.

Bad breath: "Please don't be embarrassed, Alan, this happens to everybody. But since we have the big meeting today, I thought you'd want to know that you've got a slight case of garlic breath."

Other offenses to be aware of: dandruff, greasy hair, flatulence, talking too much, interrupting, failure to wash hands in bathrooms, not covering one's mouth when coughing, and overly luxurious ear and nose hair.

These news flashes can also be passed along via anonymous notes, allowing all parties concerned to save face.

When someone pays you a compliment, what you say is this: Thank you.

Arguing with someone who is trying to pay you a compliment will only serve to make you both uncomfortable.

If you feel uncomfortable receiving praise, say, Thank you, something about how it was a team effort, and quickly divert the conversation back to the compliment giver: "Well, thanks, Bob, but you're the one who shoots five hundred yards off the tee, and by the way, great dickie!"

This display of easy modesty has the curious effect of reiterating the greatness for which you just were praised; it suggests that compliments are something to which you are very accustomed, and that, by the act of choosing to share credit, you are a leader.

things a man should know about **work**

Which reminds us: Do not accept credit for other people's brilliant ideas.

Be too busy to take credit for other people's ideas: Take initiative, be a self-starter, think about future projects.

When speaking about these projects and other projects, speak in terms of "we" rather than "I," to keep the focus on the company as a cohesive group with common goals.

When you have screwed up, do not attempt to pass the buck.

When you have screwed up, take responsibility.

When you have screwed up, your boss usually knows you have screwed up. It only causes harm to attempt to spread the blame to others, making you look like a person of no character.

When you have screwed up, say things like "I made a mistake." Then don't screw up again.

In response to a question from a higher-up, never say, "I don't know." Say, "I'll find out for you."

Brownnosing: Inappropriately attempting to curry favor with superiors by sucking up in a sycophantic, groveling fashion.

Anybody who's seen a movie or situation comedy set in a workplace knows that brownnosers always get it in the end.

ask
Mr. Etiquette Man!

Question: How is it that sycophants came to be known as toadies?

Answer: As early as the 1600's, quacks who traveled the countryside selling phony home remedies would employ an assistant to swallow a toad (widely believed poisonous) so that the quack could subsequently "revive" him with his concoctions. This person, who clearly was willing to go to great lengths to please his master, was called a toadeater.

Question: And the origin of the word "brownnosing"?

Answer: If you don't know, you're sure not going to find out here.

chapter eighteen

Dirty jokes=sexual harassment.

At one time, low-level managers frustrated by deadend jobs used to hang in their cubicles a fake sign that read, SEXUAL HARASSMENT WILL NOT BE TOLERATED—HOWEVER, IT WILL BE GRADED, a "joke" that was not funny then and is really, really not funny now.

Just in case somebody missed the memo: Sexual harassment is decidedly real.

Sexual harassment is cruel and devastating and wrong.

We mean to say that sexual harassment is serious business, and that everybody—meaning you—should regard it as such.

Fortunately, it is extraordinarily easy to avoid perpetrating sexual harassment by acting like a decent human being with just the tiniest modicum of professionalism.

Discussing someone's breasts = sexual harassment.

Repeatedly asking out someone who is not interested = sexual harassment.

Sexual harassment can involve any combination of genders.

You don't need to be the object of someone's sexual advances to be considered a victim of sexual harassment under the law.

Example: "Hostile environment" suits, in which the case is made that management ignores or permits or even condones sexually inappropriate behavior in the workplace.

Example: A person who is offended by your use of that profane word that starts with *f* can report your usage of same to the human-resources department, which is then obliged to issue a formal reprimand.

Then again, scatological words beginning in *s* do not set off those alarms.

Record judgment in the U.S. legal system in a case of sexual harassment: $34 million.

Any questions?

Moving right along . . .

things a man should know about **work**

Profanity: no.

> The previous is true even if your boss curses like a stevedore.

Cursing like a stevedore doesn't make you seem like one of the guys—it makes you seem like a stevedore.

No, we don't know what a stevedore is.

Also: Sobbing at work is to be avoided, as is singing.

It seems obvious, yet it must be said, zero racial epithets, zero ethnic insults, zero gay bashing, zero gender bashing.

These rules do not constitute so-called political correctness. The term political correctness refers to rules imposed for phony, insincere, and intellectually invalid reasons stemming from fashion or politics.

Racial-, ethnic-, sexuality-, and gender-based commentary should be avoided for valid reasons, namely because it demonstrates an unfair and unwarranted lack of respect for whole groups of people.

Racial-, ethnic-, sexuality-, and gender-based commentary also should be avoided because it can foster an environment that the groups in question consider hostile in the legal sense of the word, which can make for exciting litigation.

The previous rules apply equally to the most senior executives—such talk in the boardroom will eventually filter down to the mail room, and the mail room is the womb in which the seed of legal action finds purchase.

Again, it should be obvious, but we've all seen this maxim violated: Rules about racial-, ethnic-, sexuality-, and gender-based remarks go double in the presence of clients—especially new or prospective ones.

If for no other reason than you never know which client's mother is Polish or whose uncle is a cross-dresser or whose husband is an Evangelical Christian.

things a man should know about **work**

It goes triple where written communication such as e-mail is concerned—e-mail being traceable, storable, and reproducible.

For some of the above reasons, and also because only certain people possess the requisite talent to actually be funny, jokes are best avoided.

Regarding e-mail: Think, just for a moment, of the simple sequence of events that would cause that mash note you composed to Bootyquake5733 to instead go to your CEO.

Or to your wife.

With most e-mail programs, that sequence of events doesn't even amount to a sequence—it involves one errant keystroke.

A similar keystroke could see your proposal for a night of carnality in bunny suits carbon-copied to every employee of your company.

And those mistakes occur not just when you're talking about naughty things. You might be, say, ratting on a colleague or bragging about your job interview at a competing firm or trashing the boss or sending state secrets to Beijing—any of which in the wrong hands could take some burnish off your career.

For that and countless other legal reasons, it's best not to use e-mail for anything other than innocuous, straightforward exchanges of information: ordering staples, scheduling meetings, that sort of thing.

Most companies monitor, at least to some extent, the e-mail of their employees.

In case you haven't gotten the point yet: It might be smart "netiquette" to issue a personal blanket ban on workplace expressions regarding desires that emanate from below the beltway.

That's correct: no porn on the clock.

ask Mr. Etiquette Man!

Question: When will e-mail suffice for a thank-you note?

Answer: Not often. Mainly when you're thanking a very close friend to whom a handwritten note might seem overly formal.

Question: Is it appropriate to describe such issues as "netiquette"?

Answer: Do we refer to telephone etiquette as "phonetiquette"? To appropriate behavior on submarines as "submarinetiquette?" No. We do not.

No "spam."

No forwarding of lists or jokes or surveys or chain letters or "funny" pictures or "drawings" made with punctuation marks or executable files or anything remotely similar to the aforementioned.

Worse: sending such unsolicited material as attached files, which are in fact documents or programs that require recipients to take the extra step of downloading and opening with the proper software—and thus are even more annoying.

The message you send when you send such things: that you are a complete ass.

Also: that you've spent the last hour or two looking at joke Web sites, which is to say, that you have too much time on your hands.

things a man should know about **work**

Put another way: Think of the number of CEOs and Nobel laureates and rising star executives from whom you have received e-mails containing lists of jokes.

Yes, exactly our point.

chapter nineteen

The four p.m. sales call, wherein Mr. Jones wishes you to contemplate the merits of his company's very special manila clasp envelopes.

People who show up without appointments shall be grateful to receive an audience at all and shall not complain if a bit of waiting is involved.

Never show up without an appointment.

Never be one of those people who always make people wait whether they're truly busy or not—and you know you're out there, you nasty, nasty people.

When a person *with* an appointment must be kept waiting more than a few minutes—especially if that person is more important than you are—step out to greet her, apologize, and offer an estimate of when you'll be ready for her.

When you are ready: Apologize again and pay close attention.

You are familiar with the expression "Hold my calls"? Utilize it.

When anyone of higher rank or age enters your office, regardless of gender, you stand to greet them.

You stand to greet entering clients in particular.

You need not stand to receive colleagues of your own rank, your assistant, or other support staff when they approach your desk.

When calling on others: If you've been kept cooling your heels for twenty minutes, you may then ask the receptionist when she expects your host to be available.

When calling on a client: Don't sit on a secretary's desk.

In fact, don't sit on a secretary's anything.

When calling on others: An excellent opening salvo is, "Thank you for your time."

How to get someone out of your office: Glance at your watch and react with genuine alarm, exclaiming something along the lines of "Great horny toads—sorry to interrupt you, but I was supposed to be in a budget meeting ten minutes ago!"

And then: Thank your guest for her efforts and tell her you'll be in touch.

Wriggling out of a meeting: All assistants should be instructed in the use of an escape word, which, when uttered by the boss, brings them running to advise of an impending urgent appointment elsewhere.

Wriggling out of a meeting: Alternatively, the assistant can be instructed in advance to rescue the executive from a meeting at a prearranged time, generally with a phone call apprising her of some kind of emergency.

Better than an escape word: You know you're important when you have an emergency button under your desk.

chapter twenty

It's all about sex! In which your unjust reputation as a player is handily debunked, whether or not to be a barker, and how to bring this thing to a rollicking, if you will, climax.

The official, public version of the number of people you've slept with: half the number of people you've actually slept with.

Unless it's less than ten, in which case, say it's less than ten.

things a man should know about **sex**

Or more than 25, in which case, you are a virgin. This is your very first time. She is to be very, very gentle.

By the way, Wilt Chamberlain was full of shit.

Average age at which people lose their virginity: 16.

Average number of sexual partners in a man's life: six.

Average number of sexual partners in a woman's life: two.

Just because she acts disinterested doesn't mean she isn't interested.

When she says she is a virgin, she is most likely a virgin.

Which is to say, one inappropriate response to such an assertion would be uncontrollable laughter.

In re virginity: It is safer to leave the boldly-going-where-no-man-has-gone-before to space explorers in skintight polyester uniforms.

Then again: You could learn from a guy like Shatner, you know.

Joke: Experienced guy says to virgin, "If you want to have sex, let me know by tugging on it once. If you don't want to have sex, tug on it 379 times."

Women talk among themselves.

This point—not a theory, by the way, but an inviolate fact—foretells great peril if you're one of those missionary-only guys mentioned in the previous chapter.

things a man should know about **sex**

The result: a six-pack of Schlitz and a porn tape.

Always an option: gay sex!

We're not saying you should exercise it—merely that it's always an option.

Speaking of the love that once dared not speak its name but is now a staple of the best television sitcoms: Every guy needs a gay friend.

During your exertions, most women don't want you to be completely silent.

Some women, in fact, want you to curse like a sailor.

Others, when they hear you talk dirty, will find your attempt to impersonate an S&M daddy sort of ridiculous.

One wants to get a sense of the other's preference as regards dirty talking before one overdoes it.

Similarly, moaning, barking, shrieking, yelping.

Also yodeling. Because nobody, but nobody, really likes yodeling.

Do not moan, bark, shriek, yelp, or yodel louder than she does.

Extra Bonus Mental Picture: During his lifetime, chances are strong that the famous yodeler Slim Whitman may very well have participated in sex.

At your age, there's no such thing as a truthful woman who says, "Gee, I've never done this before."

She knows you're lying, too.

Now, then: Let's bring 'er in for a landing, here:

You are talking (a little), maybe.

You are listening (a lot), definitely.

If you violated the earlier maxim about yodeling, you are now yodeling no more.

You are focusing upon her sounds, her movements, her responses.

Because of this finely honed sensitivity, you are putting to practice the things you have learned—from her, from her predecessors, from this little book—with complete confidence, because they have become second nature to you.

Again: frequent fleeting touches of her arm, hand, back.

You are bearing in mind the fact that—how many times must the womenfolk tell us this?—the finale, the fireworks, they are not the only goal in sex.

> You are remembering (once more, with feeling): It's about her.

You'll know when.

Because she'll tell you.

Maybe not verbally, but she'll tell you.

And finish at the neck.

things a man should know about **sex**

Gauge the extent to which she desires cuddling by noting whether she is, in fact, cuddling.

Do not, under any circumstances, attempt to sing the Engelbert Humperdinck number "After the Loving" at this point.

Or any other point.

And as for "Was it good for you?"—you should never have to ask.

chapter twenty-one

Afternoon delight: sex in the workplace.

Desktop sex is a common fantasy.

The reason desktop sex is a common fantasy is its riskiness, the idea of which many people find exciting.

The aforementioned excitement quickly wilts when the boss snaps on those cold, harsh fluorescent lights—especially if you're on *her* desk.

As with most fantasies, the desktop-sex fantasy is best *kept* a fantasy—or realized atop the privacy of a desk *at home.*

In re sleeping your way to the top: Reconsider sleeping your way to the top.

Because it's actually much less difficult, let alone dangerous, to attain the top by working really hard.

When to sleep your way to the top: When your sultry, leggy, whip-crackin' dominatrix of a boss will settle for nothing less.

Note about aforementioned situation: Under such circumstances, it is really, really, *really* about her.

Even when it involves only a lateral move, as opposed to the top, interoffice "sleeping" is extremely risky.

Though riskiness is, in its own special way, sexy.

Note: Some companies' personnel departments now demand that interoffice romances be fully disclosed to them.

Those personnel people are a bored and horny lot, we're thinking.

Note: There is no kind of sexual interaction with coworkers or clients that will help your career in the long run.

Cases in point: Donna Rice, Jessica Hahn, Gennifer Flowers, Barney Frank's congressional page.

Yes, those Lewinsky handbags seem to have sold pretty well, but still.

things a man should know about **work**

Because the demands of business and the demands of pleasure quite often conflict—almost always, in fact—and when demands aren't met, the demanders can become disappointed.

Which is to say, as a general principle, sex with coworkers or clients is to be avoided.

It is also true that Americans spend a large part of their waking lives at work, and that, as such, relationships with coworkers and clients are hard to avoid.

Which means, when it comes to the office affair, you need to compartmentalize.

Try to keep it secret.

You will fail, but nonetheless, try.

One helpful technique: no public displays of affection.

Public displays of affection shall include, but not be limited to, eye batting, hand-holding, foot massaging, back rubbing, and armpit sniffing.

Point of order: Compartmentalizing one's office love affair does not mean a toss in the broom closet as opposed to a toss on the conference-room table.

What to do when the office party results in entanglement between you and a coworker: Ascertain who else knows, calculate your respective levels of regret over the situation, if applicable; slip out of the broom closet as discreetly as possible and skulk away in separate directions, never to acknowledge the incident again.

Also: There are security cameras in the elevator, and we say that not as a matter of encouragement.

The office affair involving one or more married partners: Break it off immediately.

> Exception to the former rule: If the affair is happening between you and your boss, find another job first, then break off the affair.

And remember, here, more than anywhere, the idea of respect, both for your paramour and your coworkers, is of primacy.

Right behind staying employed.

When possible, imbuing the company party with a hoedown theme shall be avoided.

How far in advance to mail invitations to an event: Cocktail party—three weeks. Dinner party, lunch or breakfast meeting—four to six weeks. Day-long conference requiring travel from other cities—up to six months.

The boss must attend the office party, even tough she'd rather not, and she must stay for a substantial period of time.

The employees must not exploit their access to the boss at a company party to sell her on their agenda or to ask for more money.

The employees must not exploit their access to the boss to inquire why she was so cheap as to hire only five belly dancers for such a big room.

How to safely juggle a plate of food and a drink at a cocktail party while also greeting people: Grow a third arm or get one of those cupholders that clamp onto the edge of your plate—yeah, that will look impressive—or get the nibbling over with quickly and carry only a drink.

things a man should know about **work**

How to avoid becoming overserved at a cocktail party: Don't drink a lot.

Strategy for not drinking a lot: Order a soda with lime and carry it until the ice melts. Repeat.

You were thinking, perhaps that this was just the time to get sauced on the company's nickel and confess your true feelings for Sherm the coffee-cart boy? Wrong.

Seriously: The arrangers of the company party must endeavor to help attendees avoid overindulgence by offering lots of food and nonalcoholic drinks and by limiting the party's length.

The arrangers also should provide for the availability of taxis.

What to do when someone who does not drink alcohol asks for a nonalcoholic drink: Supply such drink without a moment's hesitation and, most important, without any wisecracks.

It is better to provide too much food and drink than to run out of either.

This is the way it works if you're hosting clients, too.

Speaking of clients, if you've done the inviting, you do the looking after.

One does not invite clients to a strip club—at least not on company time or dime.

Even if the client wants to go.

Because her husband might be walking by when you go in.

Now, back to the looking after. The looking after includes paying for all her needs if the entertainment is out of the office, at a bar, a theater, or a sporting event, for example.

If you're the guest, it doesn't hurt to say, "Here, let me get this," the next time the peanut vendor comes round at the ball game.

If you're part of the ball game or golf game, say, there are certain virtues in sportsmanship.

Which means, no showboating, no bragging, no arguing over calls or rules.

Even if you're right.

And here's an idea for when you're playing golf with a prospective client: You let him win is what you do.

Because pride goeth before a sale.

When you are the guest, as opposed to the host, a thank-you note is mandatory.

things a man should know about **work**

chapter twenty-two

You don't bring me flowers, although you now and again come through with a Maglite.

When selecting a business gift, it's wise to think about the recipient's interests.

The opera tickets to the music buff, for example, and the Jets tickets to the jock.

Verify with other staffers that the gift you've picked is appropriate.

Better yet: Use the corporate-gift specialists on staff at most large department stores.

The corporate-gift consultant not only knows what types of gifts are most appropriate but usually can get you a corporate discount.

Everybody, male and female, likes to get flowers.

Everybody, male and female, enjoys the gift of lingerie.

Oh, behave!

For your assistant: a small, impersonal holiday gift is appropriate, for example, a small gift certificate to a department store.

An assistant who has served you loyally for a decade deserves a gift closer to the $100 area.

The supervisor does not expect to receive a gift from a subordinate.

Wine and spirits have long been traditional business gifts—just aim for a beverage that you know the recipient enjoys.

Before giving wine or spirits to a dot-com e-hole—and there's still a few of them around—make sure he is old enough to drink.

chapter twenty-three

On firing the scalawag
you just caught having
afternoon delight. On
your desk. Plus: dignity
when it's your own
head on the veritable
chopping block.

**You can't just summon a miscreant to
your office and sack him—you must
prepare.**

Why you must prepare: because the people who
decide wrongful-termination suits are the
members of juries, and there's a better-than-
average chance that people on juries are
unemployed or have recently been fired
themselves.

things a man should know about **work**

Also, if the subject in question is in the middle of a big project, make sure he has finished it and turned it in before you drop the sword, or else you'll never see the goods.

The preparation, which should be a pro-forma procedure firmly in place at your company: Procure his last check from personnel so that after he is axed, he can walk out the door immediately, never to return.

Procure also his reimbursement for unused vacation days, health-insurance information, and data on procedures for rolling over his 401(k), where applicable.

For legal purposes, establish that personnel is satisfied with your documentation of the miscreant's shortcomings.

Rather than thinking of this as personal revenge for someone's lousy performance on your watch—even if that's how you feel—try to take on an air of sympathy, compassion, and support before you cut the guy's legs out from under him.

Re the previous rule: It could prevent somebody from lunging across your desk.

It also can help the newly unemployed in the room save a little bit of face and dignity.

Don't get emotional—remember, this is business.

Remembering that this is strictly business helps one to forget about how you've just made it impossible for the poor sod to feed his three kids, pay his mortgage, and keep up with his wife's exorbitant iron-lung payments.

Also, where appropriate, have a security guard or a hefty, loyal employee nearby.

Make sure nobody in the office can hear you drop the bomb.

Good bomb-dropping language: "I think we both know this isn't working out."

> Better bomb-dropping language, considering the possibility that only *one* of you realizes things aren't working out: "This is not working out."

The idea is to not allow for discussion or argument, which can only prolong an uncomfortable situation.

Naturally, you collect all ID cards and keys from the individual, and you do not let him use his computer while cleaning out his desk—he can do major damage.

The most important advice on firing: Have someone else do it. It is an awful, nasty business, and unless you are a sadist, as one of this book's authors is, it is likely to be the worst thing that you have to do as a manager.

You can't fire me—I quit. Oh? you can? Right, then. I'll just pack up my Maglite and be on my way.

Everybody should quit a job in righteous indignation at least once.

How this is done: Step One, climb atop the boss's desk, lower trousers, and . . .

Now the proper way to quit: quietly, without smashing anything, without cursing at anyone, and with all the damaging documentation you need already carefully photocopied and stored in your home safe.

In truth, you should always produce the most upbeat letter of resignation possible—you never know when you're going to work with these people again.

If you're resigning in protest, briefly and calmly outline your reasons, then include some positive words for the company and your coworkers and close by wishing them well.

Everyone should be fired at least once.

Better that it's not you.

Should it be you, believe it or not, there are certain ways to behave.

If you are laid off as a cost-cutting measure, remain civil.

You might even write a letter thanking your supervisor for all you learned in her employ.

Because when times get better—and they usually do—you may be among the first people she calls.

So *then* you can tell her to get bent.

Which, of course, is a joke.

Because it runs counter to that oft repeated underlying principle of etiquette: Yes, the thing about respect.

Which means you treat people as you would like to be treated by them.

Which means instead of insisting that they engage in some sort of physical reworking of their anatomy, you smile.

You say, Thank you, but no thank you.

And you end it the way it all began: with a handshake.

A handshake that is, we should remind, firm, fast, and free of excess perspiration.

In fact, now that you know the things a man should know about etiquette, there should be very little perspiration at all.

things a man should know about **work**

index